RHYTHM IN THE NOVEL

RHYTHM IN THE NOVEL

BY E. K. BROWN

UNIVERSITY OF NEBRASKA PRESS • LINCOLN / LONDON

Publishers on the Plains

UNP

Copyright, Canada, 1950 by University of Toronto Press

First Bison Book printing: 1978

Most recent printing indicated by first digit below:
1   2   3   4   5   6   7   8   9   10

Library of Congress Cataloging in Publication Data

Brown, Edward Killoran, 1905–1951.
  Rhythm in the novel.

  1. Fiction—History and criticism.   2. Forster, Edward Morgan,
1879–   a passage to India.   I.   Title.
PN3365.B75   1978   808.3   77–14165
  ISBN 0–8032–1150–3
  ISBN 0–8032–6050–4 pbk.

Bison Book edition published by arrangement with the University of
Toronto Press.

Manufactured in the United States of America

TO THE MEMORY OF

W. J. ALEXANDER

1855–1944

THE ALEXANDER LECTURES

The Alexander Lectureship was founded in honour of Professor W. J. Alexander, who held the Chair of English at University College from 1889 to 1926. Each year the Lectureship brings to the University a distinguished scholar or critic to give a course of lectures on a subject related to English Literature.

NO ONE could have felt more pleasure than I did in the invitation to give the Alexander Lectures. I appreciated it as an expression of kindness and confidence from former colleagues in the Department of English at the University of Toronto, and especially from an old friend, the head of the Department in University College, Professor A. S. P. Woodhouse. He and I, both of us former students of W. J. Alexander's, were appointed to the Department exactly twenty years ago, a few months after the first series of Alexander Lectures had been delivered by my teacher and director at the Sorbonne, Louis Cazamian.

What I prized even more highly than the kindness and confidence of former colleagues was the association of this lectureship with the great man and great teacher from whom I first learned the meaning of literature and of literary study. Alexander used to say that he enjoyed music, but only as a brute beast might; and until I entered his classroom that was how I enjoyed literature. All that I can say for my state when I first encountered his teaching is that I at once appreciated how much there was to learn, and that it could be learned from him. I made a habit of something rare at Toronto, and visited his classes. There was not a series of his lectures I did not hear at least twice, and the course on nineteenth-century poets given to students in the final year of the Pass Course I heard four times. I learned from him, and still believe, that Browning, if not the greatest poet of the century, is the most interesting; and in teaching a course in Browning I still move along the track he made plain Mondays, Wednesdays, and Fridays at nine o'clock in grim Room 37, University College.

In the teaching of Browning all Alexander's powers were fully exercised. There was his power of reading aloud, in which I have never known his equal. There was his power of scrutinizing the text with the exactness and pointedness that came from his study of classical poets under Gildersleeve, who was the greatest of his teachers, and with the sanity that came from his own richness of common sense. There was his power of defining the context of a poem, in terms of his reading in history, philosophy, religion, the arts, and the sciences, his observation of nature, his travels, and his insight, sharpened and assured by humorous reflection on the vagaries of human nature. And there was another power, intimately felt by those who listened to him, and at the very centre of his teaching when he was presenting one of the writers he most cared about—Shakespeare, Burke, Wordsworth, Shelley, Carlyle, Ruskin, Browning. Great literature he believed was, to use words of Browning's, "the testimony of an especially privileged insight," which may "come in aid of the ordinary argument." A philosopher well known at Toronto has said that it is a deadly sin to seek supersubstantial nourishment from the arts. As I remember the words followed by indignant exclamation marks that Alexander used to write along the margins of my essays, I wonder whether he would have called this opinion "trash" or "nonsense" or "rubbish." Literature was a part of Alexander's religion, perhaps the most operative part: I doubt that he cared much about any theological statement but the numinous element in life was full of meaning for him.

I am not now attempting a character of Alexander—he would certainly have deplored such a use of the lectureship created to recognize his teaching. But I may as well confess that as these discourses took shape, his spirit was before my mind as his portrait was beside my table. His presence did not make composition easy—that he never did; but sometimes it saved me from the facile, the rigid, the freakish. His forefinger was raised in the old commanding gesture: I distinctly heard him use the words "trash," "nonsense," and "rubbish," and I laboured to remove the elements of offence; once or twice I think I heard him mutter an impatient "exactly," the warmest term in his lexicon of praise, but this perhaps is a delusion. More than any other lecturer on the foundation I may claim to have felt the incurable defect of all the Alexander Lectures: that they cannot be Alexander's.

Alexander's first important book, *An Introduction to the Poetry of Robert Browning* (scarcely known in Great Britain since Browning's publishers were able to prevent the import of copies on the ground that their copyright had been infringed), appeared before the poet's death. It had issued from a course given by Alexander while he held the George Munro chair of English at Dalhousie University. At a time when in most universities on this continent and in Great Britain contemporary writing was ignored and the literature of the entire nineteenth century left in a ridiculously subordinate place, Alexander developed at Toronto an honours school that was generous to the claims of both. At Johns Hopkins and in German universities he had viewed with a mixture of wonderment and contempt a scholarship that was focused on minor documents of remote periods, and without a thought of the bearing these might have on the understanding of great books and great problems. I often heard him say, and always with gusto, that his knowledge of English literature began with the accession of Henry VIII: for him the essential associations of the books he interpreted, apart from those with life itself, were with the classics, the modern literatures of France and Germany, the history and philosophy of the ancient and modern world. In his own teaching he rarely dealt except for Shakespeare with an author earlier than Dryden. With every year his interest in the books of his own time grew (he was unable, however, to do justice to the art of Joyce) and his last public lecture on a literary subject, given some years after his retirement, was on recent movements in poetry.

It seemed appropriate when a student of his gave the Alexander Lectures that the subject should be taken from the dominant genre of the nineteenth century and our own time, and that at the core there should be the work of a great living English writer.

The lectures are printed substantially as they were delivered: I have removed a number of local references, but have not otherwise adapted them to a more general public.

Permissions to quote have been kindly given by the following: Edward Arnold & Co. and Harcourt, Brace & Company, Inc., for quotations from *Aspects of the Novel* and *A Passage to India* by E. M. Forster; William Heinemann, Ltd., and Mr. W. Somerset Maugham for a quotation from *Cakes and Ale,* by Mr. Maugham; Alfred A. Knopf for a quotation from *The Professor's*

House, by Willa Cather; Macmillan & Co., Ltd., for a quotation from *The Well-Beloved,* by Thomas Hardy.

For much kindness during the week when I held the lectureship, as at many other times, it is a pleasure to express my thanks to the members of the University of Toronto, especially to the President, Sidney E. Smith, to the former President, H. J. Cody, to the Principal of University College, W. R. Taylor, and to my former colleagues in the Department of English, R. S. Knox, E. J. Pratt, and A. S. P. Woodhouse.

E. K. B.

CONTENTS

PHRASE, CHARACTER, INCIDENT, *Page one* · EXPANDING SYMBOLS, *Page thirty-one* · INTERWEAVING THEMES, *Page sixty-one* · RHYTHM IN E. M. FORSTER'S *A PASSAGE TO INDIA, Page eighty-seven* · INDEX, *Page one hundred and seventeen*

I

PHRASE, CHARACTER, INCIDENT

N *The Craft of Fiction* Percy Lubbock describes the plight from which no reader of novels can quite escape. "As quickly as we read, [the novel] melts and shifts in the memory; even at the moment when the last page is turned, a great part of the book, its finer detail, is already vague and doubtful." When the reader of novels turns critic, as in some degree every good reader does, what is the object he criticizes? It is not the novel he has laid aside but rather the fragments of it that have lodged in his memory. Some of these fragments remain not because of intrinsic importance but simply because they hook on to something in his mind. From *En route* I recall the church in which Luc Durtal was happiest because it is the church of Saint-Sévérin where I assisted at midnight mass the first year I was in Paris. But I do not recall, unless I turn to the text of Huysmans, a number of the crucial incidents in the plot of the book, still less the order in which these incidents have been so carefully set. How enviable the connoisseur of painting who, in one glance at the *Primavera* of Botticelli—not the first glance, of course—can apprehend the relationships and other beauties in the picture, and can set down his impressions, the entire object enchanting and complete before his eyes! How enviable the critic of lyric who has so little chance to forget before his ear and eye and mind have done with the last syllable of

"In Time of 'The Breaking of Nations'" and he can begin to express what it has signified for him! In comparison what we may say of *War and Peace* or *Don Quixote*, of even so short a novel as *Le Père Goriot*, is merely approximation. We shall never say exactly the right thing. Perhaps it is because great critics have appreciated the inevitable flaw in all that is said about novels that they have seldom written about them. To keep to English names, how little has been said about prose fiction by Johnson and Coleridge and Arnold and Pater!

The best writing about novels has usually come from novelists, in such pieces as the prefaces and other critical writings of Henry James and Thomas Mann, and a book with which I shall be much concerned in these discourses, E. M. Forster's *Aspects of the Novel*. The novelist who practises criticism carefully, as James and Mann and Forster have, is the best guide there is. But he is an imperfect guide. As Zola frankly admitted of his own papers on the novel, the novelist who turns to criticism is always more or less intent on clearing the path for the right reception of his own kind of novels, and will produce not equitable and balanced studies but *la critique du combat*. Somerset Maugham makes the point amusingly through the narrator in *Cakes and Ale*:

A little while ago I read in the *Evening Standard* an article by Mr. Evelyn Waugh in the course of which he remarked that to write novels in the first person [as Somerset Maugham so often and so happily does] was a contemptible practice. I wish he had explained why, but he merely threw out the statement with just the same take-it-or-leave-it casualness as Euclid used when he made his celebrated observation about parallel straight lines. I was much concerned and forthwith asked Alroy Kear (who reads everything, even the books he writes prefaces for) to recommend to me some works on the art of fiction. On his advice I read *The Craft of Fiction* by Mr. Percy Lubbock, from which I learned that the only way to write novels was like Henry James; after that I read *Aspects of the Novel* by Mr. E. M. Forster, from which I learned that the only way to write novels was like Mr. E. M. Forster. . . .

Cakes and Ale came out in 1930; I wish it might have been delayed ten years; for the narrator's list might then have continued, "After that I read *The Summing Up* by Mr. W. Somerset Maugham, from which I learned that the only way to write novels was like Mr. Somerset Maugham."

For my part I am grateful that Mr. Maugham gave us his recipe for the mixture as before, as I am grateful that other novelists have done the same. When in the end someone writes that treatise on the nature of the novel comparable with the *Poetics*, ideas from James, Mann, Forster, yes, and Maugham too, will be woven into it; but the substance of that work will not come wholly, or largely, from the criticism or from the practice of any one novelist or school.

In the meantime at least three kinds of critical studies can I believe help the reader of novels: to say what might help the writer of novels is beyond my scope. Most important of the three is the sort of work that Percy Lubbock and E. M. Forster have done—a gathering and sifting of the impressions and opinions about the novel acquired in years of reading novels, writing novels, and writing about novels. Then there is another kind of critical book, of which I cannot name an example—the rounded analysis and estimate of a great novel by a critic both firm and sensitive. Our habits of reading are against the ripening of books with so narrow a range. One of the most illuminating remarks I remember was overheard at a public examination for the

licentiate in English at the Sorbonne. The examiner was
Emile Legouis. He asked a young man for his impressions of education at English and American universities.
The student replied that what had impressed him most
was the amount of reading expected and accomplished.
"Yes," said Legouis, "yes, they read, read, read." He was
silent for a full minute. "It would appear," he mused,
"that they find something magical in reading." But there
is nothing magical in reading: it is in rereading that
some magic may lie. Our habits as students, as teachers,
as simple readers for simple pleasure, are not those of
rereaders. We are open to the rebuke with which Sterne
breaks into *Tristram Shandy*: "How could you, Madame, be so inattentive in reading the last chapter?"
We are like that poor woman he invents to abuse,
"whose vicious taste, which has crept into thousands
besides herself," induced her to read "straight forwards
in quest of the adventures"; and we do not repair our
injustice to the author by rereading his work when,
knowing what the adventures are, and how they turn
out, we can attend to his effects. We read and then instead of rereading we read around. The person who is
captivated by *Wuthering Heights* reads everything the
other Brontës wrote, even the unreadable novels of the
Reverend Patrick Brontë. He reads all the books mentioned in Charlotte's letters. If the curates at Haworth
had published their sermons, he would read them.
Meanwhile he has probably forgotten the importance
to the novel of that imaginary sermon of the Reverend
Jabes Branderham, on the theme "Seventy Times Seven,
and the First of the Seventy-First." Yet every time
Wuthering Heights is reread it releases a little more of
its mysterious meaning.

There is a third kind of critical study, to which I hope these lectures may belong. Isolating a single element or group of elements in the novel, and considering it in unreal separation from all the other elements with which it actually fuses, is artificial, but so is all criticism. The artificiality is justified if when one turns back from the criticism to the novels these appear more intelligible and more delightful. That is the test. You need a great many lamps, some of them very powerful, to find your way through the labyrinth of a great novel. I offer what is perhaps only a candle, and I hope it may not go out.

Eight pages in E. M. Forster's *Aspects of the Novel* led me into thinking about the various forms rhythm may take and the various effects it may produce. As a preliminary definition of rhythm a phrase of his will serve: rhythm is "repetition with variation." In itself this phrase has no great precision. Unlimited variation is inconceivable in fiction, or anywhere else in art: a work of fiction nearing the possible limit becomes more and more nonsensical, as in these lines from an early story of Elliot Paul's:

> The Little Grey Home in the West
> The Calf of Gold
> Mumbo Jumbo
> Abd el Krim
> Robert E. Lee and George Sand
> The Bicycle Railroad
> Swedenborg
> Zinovieff
> Lord Kitchener
> Who's Who in South Dakota

Repetition without variation is conceivable. Leopold Bloom, who is somewhat given to this form of discourse, reflects: "Pray for us. And pray for us. And pray for us.

Good idea the repetition." Is it? Litanies are repetitive, but with variations: the plea to pray for us is not repeatedly addressed to the same person, or else, on the rare occasions when it is, the person is addressed under several aspects. Between exact repetition and unlimited variation lies the whole area of significant discourse and significant form.

I am concerned with but a small part of that area, the part where repetition is exceptionally strong, and variation is related to it in some fashion especially artful, pleasing, or powerful. Aldous Huxley allows the novel-writing character in *Point Counter Point* to reflect on variation in prose fiction. Among Philip Quarles's jottings in his notebook are these sentences: "A novelist modulates by reduplicating situations and characters. He shows several people falling in love, or dying, or praying in different ways—dissimilars solving the same problem. Or, *vice versa*, similar people confronted with dissimilar problems." Both sorts of variation appear effectively in *Point Counter Point*; but I do not think that either is as important to the structure of that novel as a device in which repetition outweighs the variations that are linked to it. The novel opens on a crisis in the life of Walter Bidlake, who turns from the bloodless Marjorie Carling to the predatory Lucy Tantamount. Walter's story is a prelude for the story of his sister, Elinor, the main action of the novel. Elinor turns from the bloodless Philip Quarles towards the predatory Everard Webley. Both Walter and Elinor are fearfully hurt, although not in the same way, by the entrance into their lives of the predatory characters. At the core of the novel one finds not similar people confronted with dissimilar problems, not dissimilar people solving the same problem, but similar people confronted by the same problem. Repetition is the dominant device; still if Walter and Elinor are similar, they are not the same, they do not duplicate each other, and the shades of variation, although secondary, are essential to the effect that Aldous Huxley achieves.

In this first discourse the kinds of repetition with variation will be very simple, combinations of word and phrase, sequences of incident, groupings of character. In the second discourse a more complex combination will come up—the growth of a symbol as it accretes meaning from a succession of contexts. In the third discourse themes will appear interweaving, and in doing so repeating and varying in an interactive relationship. In the fourth discourse, all the kinds of rhythm noticed before will return, coexisting, and taking on added beauty and power from the coexistence, in the latest (but, I continue to hope, not the last) of E. M. Forster's novels.

II

For an example of the simplest kind of repetition, uncomplicated by the least variation, I turn to *Middlemarch*, to one of its minor characters, the uncle of Dorothea and Celia, Mr. Brooke of Tipton. George Eliot comments on "his usual tendency to say what he had said before"; and informs us, superfluously, that "this fundamental principle of human speech was markedly exhibited in Mr. Brooke." His speeches are streaked with "well, now's" and "you know's"; with things that "will not do" and things he had "gone into at one time, up to a certain point." Most of Mr. Brooke's remarks are but faintly amusing, if amusing at all, when they are first made; it is the repetition that makes them so great a pleasure. As Maurice Bardèche has said of characters in the Waverley novels, "the comedy resides in the recurrence in each personage of his constant preoccupation." Mr. Brooke's discourse is an excellent instance of that verbal repetition for comic effect studied by Bergson in *Le Rire,* and noted by Mr. Stoll in his searching essay on "The Comic Method." Mr. Stoll describes the repetitious comic character as having "his utterance reduced to the laconic squeak of a mechanical toy." Mr. Brooke, it happens, is anything but laconic; his range of squeaks is, however, a small one; and once we have learned to know the range it would be a disappointment if he squeaked otherwise. Our laughter depends on our feeling that what Mr. Brooke says is determined not by the stimulus that sets him talking, but by the hard moulds in his mind, moulds from which he can no more escape than the jack-in-the-box can alter his squeak.[1]

I began with Mr. Brooke because the comic effect George Eliot achieves through him depends almost exclusively on repetition. He arouses heartier and heartier laughter as the novel advances and the repetitive device is worked more and more vigorously. Jane Austen's Mr. Woodhouse, Uncle Toby, Mr. Micawber are finer cases

[1]Mr. Brooke's repetitiveness of speech is the means by which his political ambitions are ruined. When he addresses the electors of Middlemarch, being slightly drunk he is more repetitive than usual. As he comes to some particularly absurd repetitions an effigy of him is hoisted above the crowd that faces him, and from below there rises "like the note of a cuckoo a parrot-like Punch-voiced echo of his words." Amid laughter he is forced to give up speaking; and that is the end of his political career. His opponents had recognized that repetitiveness was as inevitable in his discourse as the squeak is with a jack-in-the-box.

of verbal repetition; but none of them is so nearly a pure case. The strain of repetition is only one, and that not at all the most important, of the devices by which Mr. Micawber's idiom becomes the prodigy it is. Mr. Brooke, as a comic character, is a repeater, and not much else.

Verbal repetition complicated, enriched, by variation, is used very strikingly by George Moore in *Esther Waters*. That novel opens with a picture of Esther waiting at a country station for a direction to Woodview, the great house where she has been engaged as a kitchen maid:

> She stood on the platform watching the receding train. The white steam curled above the few bushes that hid the curve of the line, evaporating in the pale evening. A moment more and the last carriage would pass out of sight, the white gates at the crossing swinging slowly forward to let through the impatient passengers.

That is the first paragraph, a painter's rendering of the place and the moment. It is the painter who rules the next paragraph also, rendering Esther's oblong box, painted reddish brown; her faded yellow dress, and her black jacket too warm for the season; her short strong arms, plump neck, nose thick and fleshy but with well-formed nostrils, almond-shaped teeth, grave almost sullen face that it was a pleasure to see when it lit up with sunny humour. Esther is twenty.

The rest of the chapter follows her on the walk to Woodview, past the neat semi-detached villas close to the station, by the lodge and a gate-keeper playing the flute, along an avenue of elms, where Esther pauses to ask a young man if she is in the right way. William Latch likes her on sight, and takes her to the great house, with its elaborate gardens, its shining windows, and the bustle of servants in the kitchen.

Esther lives eighteen years of her life before us. The years at the country house, good years, end with dismissal because she is to have an illegitimate child by William Latch. In London she endures years of overwork, exploitation, humiliation. These are followed by a second span of good years, also in London, in the service of a kindly woman writer. Then Esther meets William again, stays with him through years that are a prosaic domestic mixture of good and bad, until he dies, all his money gone.

The first paragraph of chapter XLIV, within view of the end of the novel, is the same as the first paragraph of chapter I, word for word. But in what follows there is variation. If the station platform is the same, and the moment of the day, Esther is the same only in small part. Moore cannot repeat most of what he had said about her. The oblong box, painted reddish brown, is still with her. Her clothes are again worn—she has a dingy skirt—and again unsuited to the season; but now it is because they are too thin, not too warm, for the season is November. Of the well-formed nostrils and the almond-shaped teeth there is not a word; and we are to take it that what beauty Esther had had, disappeared with youth. At twenty her neck was plump; now she is stout and strongly built. The second passage ends with a remark on the "blunt outline" of her face and on the grey eyes which reflect "all the natural prose of the Saxon." Now there is no smile to soften the outline or light up the eyes.

And the walk to Woodview is the same only in small part. The neat villas are unchanged; but the lodge is

empty, and there is no flute playing gate-keeper. The
elms have been neglected, and one lies where it has
fallen. There is no young man to point the way through
the gardens which have become a wild tangle. The
windows of Woodview are shuttered. One old woman
lives there, and Esther is to be her one servant. In that
bustling kitchen the fire is out.

"Here she was," says Moore, superfluously, "back at
the very point from which she started." The circularity
is obvious; but neither Esther nor the point is quite the
same. Both have declined in the same way; both are
in the last phase. The heir will not restore Woodview;
and Esther will not meet another William Latch.

Moore's word for word repetition shading off into a
most artificially arranged set of variations is just as
blunt, just as mechanical, a device as Mr. Brooke's
repetitive speech. I would not claim for Moore's art, as
I did not claim for George Eliot's, that it was a fine
case of the effect required: but like hers it is a pure
case, a conspicuous case, and so an excellent example.

III

Neither Moore nor George Eliot, in the verbal arti-
fices with which it seemed simplest to begin, was so
audaciously emphatic as Hardy in the sequence of incidents in a novel almost contemporary with *Esther
Waters*, *The Well-Beloved*. Hardy is working here with
the theme of *Epipsychidion*, a man in love with an ideal
of woman which flits from one body to another from his
youth to the end of his life. The sub-title, as so often
with Hardy, tells as much as the title or more: it is *A
Sketch of a Temperament*. Jocelyn Pierston at twenty

falls in love with a girl of his own years, Avice Caro.
.Nearing forty he falls in love with her daughter, who
appears the very duplicate (or in the rich Wessex
speech "the daps") of what her mother had been in
youth. At past sixty he falls in love once more, and lest
I seem to pervert the sense of the novel, to over-stress
the hard mould of repetition which shapes the narrative,
I must give the conversation in which Pierston explains
his amorous history to this love of his elder years:

"Since it is well you should know all the truth before we go
any further," he said as they sat down, "that there may be no
awkward discoveries afterwards, I am going to tell you something about myself—if you are not too distressed to hear it?"
"No,—let me hear it."
"I was once the lover of your mother, and wanted to marry
her; only she wouldn't, or rather couldn't, marry me."
"O how strange!" said the girl, looking from him to the
breakfast things, and from the breakfast things to him. "Mother
has never told me that. Yet of course you might have been. I
mean, you are old enough."
He took the remark as a satire she had not intended. "O yes—
quite old enough," he said grimly. "Almost too old."
"Too old for mother? How's that?"
"Because I belonged to your grandmother."
"No? How can that be?"
"I was her lover likewise. I should have married her if I had
gone straight on instead of round the corner."
"But you couldn't have been, Mr. Pierston! You are not old
enough? Why, how old are you?—you have never told me."
"I am very old."
"My mother's, and my grandmother's," said she, looking at
him no longer as at a possible husband, but as a strange fossilized
relic in human form. Pierston saw it, but meaning to give up
the game he did not care to spare himself.
"Your mother's and your grandmother's young man," he repeated.
"And were you my great-grandmother's too?" she asked, with
an expectant interest in his case as a drama that overcame her
personal considerations for a moment.

The passage that I quote cannot be read without laughter; nor do I think the laughter is the saturnine philosophical laughter evoked by some of Hardy's lyrics, the laughter that I should be tempted to call ironic if I were quite sure I could attach a clear meaning to that epithet. No, it is in part the laughter of farce, the laughter that is evoked by what Mr. Stoll has called "mechanical *raideur*." The incidents in Hardy's novel give out the same sort of expected squeak that marked Mr. Brooke's discourse. Yet the theme of *Epipsychidion* was one that Hardy brooded and gloomed over, and in this novel there are many passages so grave and sympathetic that much as I should like to accept Mr. Joseph Warren Beach's suggestion that one take the book as "all good fun" it cannot be written off in that way. The history of the book is proof that Hardy soon knew he had not accomplished the effect he intended: five years passed between the serial and the novel, and *The Well-Beloved* has never been reprinted except in editions of the collected novels. Repetition was plied so hard, so inflexibly that what might have been a serious and delicate philosophical fantasy hardened into outlines as rigid as those of the stones that Pierston's father cut. It is true that, looked at closely, the three women who count most heavily in Pierston's life do not wholly repeat one another. They differ in temperament and in intelligence. He loses them in different ways. Their after-histories are different. But these and other variations in the incidents and in the characters scarcely affect the reader's response, so emphatic, so essential is the repetition.

One important dissimilarity between the verbal repetitions of George Eliot and Moore, and the repetition of incident and character in *The Well-Beloved,* is that Hardy's use of the device shapes his plot, where Moore's and George Eliot's does not. Mr. Brooke's mechanical *raideur* undoubtedly affects the plot of *Middlemarch*: not only does it become the tool by which his political career is frustrated, it accounts in part for his failure to take in the tragic folly of a marriage between Dorothea and Dr. Casaubon and to prevent or at least postpone it. Moore's effect of circularity supplies a moving reinforcement for the meaning of his plot. Still verbal repetitiveness, with or without variation, cannot have very much to do with plot. As I set beside the pure verbal repetitiveness of George Eliot, the blending in verbal terms of repetition with variation in *Esther Waters,* I shall now set beside the pure repetitiveness of incident in *The Well-Beloved* some parts of *The Old Wives' Tale* where emphatic repetition penetrates into the plot, and yet is balanced by liberal variations.

The first incident in *The Old Wives' Tale* presents the Baines girls, Sophia and Constance, in their middle teens, looking from the window on the family's middle-aged drudge, Maggie. Maggie is meeting her follower, and clearly she is in love. All the disagreeable things the girls say to each other about Maggie's being in love come out of a single limitation in their natures—that they are young, and know nothing more of what it means to be middle-aged than, well, than Sophocles knew of the cathedral of Chartres. Bennett repeats the incident after a lapse of eight years, when Sophia, at twenty-three, has seen a great deal and suffered more. She is in the apartment of Madame Foucault, a middle-aged *demi-mondaine* who has nursed her through an illness of which she almost died. Madame Foucault has been spurned by her *ami*, and is sobbing on the floor. To Sophia her love-lorn state is as absurd and as repulsive as Maggie's had been. A few months later Bennett involves Sophia in a situation that does not repeat the two I have mentioned, but is closely linked with them. An old man asks her to become his mistress: she is not much offended morally, nor is she horrified; she is simply angry that the old man is not behaving like her *cliché* of an old man; to her older people still belong to a different species. "Do not," she says to him, "be an old fool."

In an incident set very near the end of Sophia's life Bennett directly repeats the substance of the first of his incidents, but with a reversal of roles. Sophia and Constance, women of sixty, have taken a young maid who has masterful ways. Maud is exuberantly youthful: she delights in wrangles, noises, drafts, and almost everything that older people detest. She has the most unimaginative ignorance of the exact kind of nervous tremors she gives the two old women, it is another case of Sophocles and the cathedral of Chartres. But now, and for the first time in Sophia's life, it is from the older person's point of view we follow an incident that sets young against old. Bennett manages a most moving and troubling effect, in which our memories of the earlier incidents in this series jostle with our impressions of the page we read. One difference between Bennett's manipulation of the device and Hardy's is that Bennett avoids the stiffening of repetition into mere formula: he knows how variation works in what I shall now begin to call the rhythmic process, the combination of the repeated and the variable with the repeated as the ruling factor. Another difference is that if repetition does penetrate into the narrative of *The Old Wives' Tale*, it does not shape the plot. No turn in the affairs of Constance and Sophia follows from their contempt for Maggie in love, or from Sophia's contempt for Madame Foucault, or from her spurning of the old boarder, or from Maud's contempt for Sophia and Constance. The repetitive incidents are simply illustrative: suggesting an immutable order, they do not reduce all else to it.

Still, if repetition is not as emphatic in *The Old Wives' Tale* as in *The Well-Beloved*, it is conspicuous. It was introduced with unmistakable calculation, employed with an attempt as deliberate and almost as mechanical as Moore's to enforce a theme. Is there not a finer, more flexible use of the rhythmic process in incident?

It is extraordinary the number of Thackeray's readers who forget how *Vanity Fair* ends. When I first taught it, as an instructor in this University, and was reading it for the third or perhaps the fourth time, and barely keeping abreast of the class, I needed unexpectedly to refer to the end of the book; to my exasperation I could not recall whether Becky died, or whether she again vanished into the abyss as she had done after Rawdon Crawley drove her from his house, or whether she disappeared in the midst of some minor reverse. I am sympathetic to H. B. Lathrop who says she ended in "dirty squalor,"[1] and to that discriminating interpreter of Thackeray's art, Charles Whibley. Whibley says: "[Becky Sharp] shows a fine spirit of gaiety and courage

[1] Lathrop claims that Thackeray was "indifferent to the endings" of his novels, and thus prepares for his own slip.

in the sombre atmosphere of Pumpernickel. 'She was at home with everybody in the place—pedlars, punters, tumblers, students, and all.' Though her adversaries were meaner, and the stakes lower, she was still playing the same game of life, which she played against the Marquis of Steyne, and, after her fashion, she was a winner to the end." But Pumpernickel is not the end. It is admirably drawn, and no one is likely to forget the seedy attic bedroom, No. 92, in the Elephant Inn, with the frowsy student bawling his love through the keyhole, and inside, Becky Sharp, the rouge pot, the brandy bottle, and the plate of broken meat in the bed. Thackeray did not take leave of Becky in these lively if squalid surroundings; he took leave of her at Bath and Cheltenham, where she was not a winner to the end after her fashion, or anyone's, where she sued year after year, and with only fair success, for acceptance by a society of dreary dowagers.[1] These women, among whom her history ends, would have enjoyed the women with whom her history begins, her teachers, the Misses Pinkerton. The greater Miss Pinkerton should have retired to Bath or Cheltenham: she would have found there the perfect audience for her story of the Great Lexicographer's visit which had made the fortune of her academy. Becky's history begins with the defiance of respectable folk, the hurling of the Great Lexicographer's "dixonary" from the carriage that is whirling her away from the Pinkertons' fortress of respectability. She needs nearly twenty years to learn that she cannot pay the cost of defying respectability. Her history has a beautiful circularity, which is the more satisfying since Becky at the end is exactly the same in impulse as she had

[1] In *The Newcomes*, chap. XXIII, Becky has turned to writing hymns.

been twenty years before. We are sure that she would like to hurl the prayer book, exhibited so ostentatiously before the dowagers, in the face of the congregation, and dash away in a carriage, preferably with a coronet. The circularity is the more striking because of the likeness between what followed Becky's leaving the Pinkertons and what preceded, and indeed made possible, the sojourns at Bath and Cheltenham. From the Pinkertons Becky went with her dearest Amelia to the Sedley house, and there at once set about her first scheme—to get possession of Jos Sedley and his money. She failed. Her tale is one of a thousand and one schemes; but the first and the last of her schemes are exactly the same. It is by getting possession of Jos Sedley and his money that she extricates herself from the squalor of Bohemia, from the punters and pedlars and students of Pumpernickel. Free of Jos—did she kill him? no doubt we are intended to say she did—and with his money safe in her clutch, she takes the veil of respectability. The variations of Thackeray, working with a flexibility and a sense for the soft and indistinct contours of life that none of the writers considered before him could approach, render his effect much less emphatic. Perhaps it is not quite emphatic enough; for in missing the circularity of Becky's history H. B. Lathrop and Charles Whibley—and how many others?—have misread his novel.

IV

These examples of rhythmic incident and situation depend on a sequence in time; but there is another form of the rhythmic process that essentially does not, the kind that Balzac uses in *Le Père Goriot*. It has been

said that Père Goriot is a Lear without a Cordelia;[1] it
is no less true that his daughters, Anastasie and Delphine, are more formidably alike than Regan and
Goneril. If you were to meet them at one of the balls
for which they live they would not seem to be of the
same stuff: Anastasie is dark and Delphine fair; Anastasie married for rank and has almost the manners of
the Faubourg Saint-Germain (though she does not live
in it), Delphine married for money and has the manners
of a banker's wife from the Chaussée d'Antin. If you
listened to the scandal about them, it would not tell the
same story: Anastasie was thought to give money to her
lover, Delphine to take it from hers. None of these
variations touches the core of the characters. Nor does
the difference in their roles in the history of Eugène de
Rastignac. He first lays siege to Anastasie and is making
excellent progress until he ventures a clumsy reference
to her father. He turns then to Delphine, and with her
he does not fail. The outcome is different not because
the daughters are, but—here there is a sequence in time
—because Eugène knows far more about Paris when
he approaches Delphine than he had known when he
made his first call on Anastasie and blundered.

The daughters are alike at the core, the very same indeed, because they are the products of the same circumstance, the deplorable upbringing their idolatrous
father gave them. Not only has Goriot no Cordelia; as
Balzac reads character he could not have had a Cor-

[1]Balzac introduces a Cordelian character, Victorine Taillefer, who
is treated as cruelly by her father as Goriot by his daughters. The
inversion of roles in the sub-plot of the Taillefers is a repetition with
variation comparable with the relation between the Baines sisters
and their servants except that in Le Père Goriot the inversion is not
in a time sequence.

delia, unless, by some blessed chance, she had been exchanged at birth and reared by a wiser hand. Anastasie and Delphine make the same kinds of demand on their father; and put the same kind of humiliation on him. Only so can Balzac render his theme with the fullest emphasis, and prevent the reader's escaping from the impact he intends. If Père Goriot had had only one ravenously selfish daughter, the reader might have said: "No, it was not her upbringing that ruined her, there was something ineradicably corrupt inside her for which her father was not answerable. He is guiltless." But if there are two ravenously selfish daughters, and no others, and if they are selfish in exactly the same way, the guilt is fixed elsewhere.[1]

We see the Goriot daughters as we see everyone, through Eugène's eyes. Anastasie rejects him; Delphine is kind to him. He treasures every least indication that she may be softer than her sister, that her exploitation of her father has extenuations, if not a justification, in the special ugliness of her husband's nature. If neither daughter comes to Goriot's deathbed until he has sunk into the final coma, it is Anastasie who comes before he dies, and what she says is merciless to herself, but Delphine does not come at all. Eugène's eyes are quite open now: the line he had insisted on drawing between Delphine and Anastasie was a lover's illusion. Anastasie was not really altered by her sudden insight into her own wickedness. Neither daughter comes to see Goriot

[1]In Miss I. Compton-Burnett's *Two Worlds and Their Ways* the same repetitive device is used, and its significance is pointed for us by the father, Sir Roderick Shelley. When Sir Roderick learns that in their first school term both his son and his daughter have cheated he declares, "The fact that the result was the same with them both shows that it came from something outside." Like Goriot he was to blame for the performance of his children; unlike Goriot he saw and admitted the truth at once.

in his coffin; and neither comes to his funeral. If for a moment near the end of the story Delphine appeared to be even harder than her sister, it was for a moment only. Their absence from the funeral rivets them together again.

Another telling of the Lear story, again with no Cordelia, introduces the sort of calculated variation observed in Bennett's art, but here exercised not on a series of incidents, but on a pair of characters, a marking of what Fielding who set a high value on it calls "the nice distinction between two persons actuated by the same vice." The hero in Turgenev's *A Lear of the Steppes,* the landowner Martin Petrovitch Harlov, a mountain of a man, has like Goriot lost his wife very early, and like Goriot has two daughters. Anna, the elder, is slight, with thin features; her lips are thin and cruel, and her hand thin and "malignant." The narrator, a boy living on the next estate, never has the least doubt about Anna; she has charm, but an evil nature. Evlampia is like her father: she is tall, stout, and fair; it is true that she has a wild fierce eye, but so has he, and the narrator likes him as we do. Harlov signs over his estate to his daughters, and both at once turn upon him. In the great scene of the novel, one of the most terrifying scenes in fiction, Harlov, standing on the roof of the house that once was his, tears off the boards, and wrenches the bricks from the chimney. Evlampia prevents him from being shot by her sister's greedy husband, and assures him of her love and remorse. Harlov, as he tries to pull down a standard, falls to the ground, and as he dies he stammers to Evlampia the enigmatic words: "Well, daughter . . . you I do not . . . ." Opinion in the neighbourhood in the days after Harlov's death drew a line between Evlampia and

Anna. Both were guilty, but only Anna was shunned. The boy was absorbed by the question whether the old man had intended not to curse or not to forgive Evlampia.[1] Not to curse, he decided, and I think a reader is persuaded of this. The two girls have been rendered with such a delicate difference: both were harsh; but Evlampia was harsh in her father's fashion, and since he can be so kind and so decent, we are ready to think she could be kind and decent, although she never was before the scene when she implored her father to come down. *A Lear of the Steppes* has an epilogue. Fifteen years after Harlov's death, the narrator returns to the neighbourhood. He sees and talks with Anna. She is precisely what we expected she would become, a hard cruel landowner, happy in her hardness, all of a piece. Then, four years later, he sees Evlampia, who had left the estate immediately after her father's death and never returned. She is thin now, and her expression has changed to sternness, pride, and the "satiety of power." She is chief mother in a sect of Flagellant dissenters. That is the last note in the story, a note so bold and strong that a reader must feel with the novelist that it will endure no prolongation.

Turgenev makes his effect in *A Lear of the Steppes* by a combination of gradation with surprise. Gradation —the cruel Anna, so obviously and eternally cruel, and Evlampia cruel at first only in an unemphatic and spasmodic way, and then revealed as monstrously, orgiastically cruel. There is the surprise.

Perhaps it was from Turgenev that Henry James

---

[1]In the original, Harlov's last speech breaks after the first syllable of a word which might have been *proklinzaiu* (curse) or *proshtchaiu* (forgive).

learned the art of arranging characters by gradation and combining with it surprise. It is James's mastery of gradation that E. M. Forster is neglecting when he complains of the fewness of the types of character that furnish the novels of James. "He has," says Forster, "a very short list of characters. . . . the observer who tries to influence the action, and the second-rate outsider. . . . Then there is the sympathetic foil, very lively and frequently female . . . there is the wonderful rare heroine . . . there is sometimes a villain, sometimes a young artist with generous impulses; and that is about all. For so fine a novelist it is a poor show." It is a short list; but is it a poor show?

In *The Ambassadors,* the novel Mr. Forster examines, there is a young artist with generous impulses, Little Bilham, who has left America to study in Paris. In and about the ateliers he discovers that he has no talent for art, but a distinguished faculty for enjoying artistic and civilized company, the kind of company that Henry James preferred to that of poets and philosophers and would have preferred to that of archangels if he had believed in them. Little Bilham sets his course so that his distinguished faculty may develop and be exercised; he has the dignity of self-knowledge and simple consistency. As the observer who tries to influence the action—in *The Ambassadors* this is Lambert Strether, the elderly New Englander—approaches a building in the Boulevard Malesherbes, he sees Little Bilham smoking on a balcony. He had hoped he might see another young man, Chad Newsome, whose balcony this is, and whom it is Strether's mission to rescue from the wickedness of Europe and ship home to his mother and the manufacturing town of Woollett, Massachusetts.

Strether has not seen Chad for over five years; but he
quickly appreciates that much as Chad may have
changed he cannot have changed so much as to have
become the little man on the balcony. For the rest of the
novel we are invited to measure Chad by Little Bilham.
At first the comparison is all to Chad's advantage. Of the
two young men who have come to Paris from America
and enjoy there the best of artistic and civilized
company, Chad seems by so much the more impressive.
He is charming to look at; he is at the centre of the
company, and Little Bilham seems only a permitted
attendant spirit; and above all it is Chad who is loved
by the rare and wonderful heroine of the novel, Madame
de Vionnet. Chad has it all his own way. But we begin
to make disturbing discoveries about Chad. He has not
the dignity of self-knowledge, or the simple consistency
of Little Bilham; he has been refined and polished by
Madame de Vionnet, but the material was not of the first
order, and the polish and refinement are not durable—
they chip off. The appeal of the large sums of money to be
made at Woollett grows stronger; and Chad grows tired
of Madame de Vionnet, for with her he is living above
his natural level. His shortcomings, his confusions, his
inconsistencies appear in a scene that comes near the
end of the novel, a scene on the same balcony of the
building in the Boulevard Malesherbes. Strether and
he come to grips smoking there; and the reader is
helped to see what is amiss in Chad by his memory of
the figure that had stood smoking on that balcony when
Strether approached it for the first time.

There is gradation no less effective in the relationship
between Chad and Strether. At first they appear totally
unlike: the only things they have in common are their

roots in New England, their respect for Mrs. Newsome and relation to her, and their presence in Paris. Strether responds with a gradual intensity to the appeal of the artistic and civilized company; and beginning as Mrs. Newsome's ambassador, urging Chad to sail for home, he shifts to become Madame de Vionnet's ambassador, urging him to stay in Paris. He becomes Chad's peer in the appreciation of Europe, and then his superior. He achieves Little Bilham's self-knowledge and simple consistency.

Each of these persons irradiates the others, and each becomes clearer by irradiation. By this irradiation the Jamesian scene assumes the soft contours of life that Thackeray achieved by his beautiful flexibility. The grouping of characters by gradation enables James to draw from that "short list" of his a show that is very far from being a poor one. James's rhythmic use of gradation does not make for strength and boldness as Turgenev's does, but the strength and boldness come from his complementary use of antithesis—Mrs. Newsome set over against Madame de Vionnet, Waymarsh the American success set over against Gloriani the European success, Mamie Pocock the nubile girl of the American ruling class versus Jeanne de Vionnet the perfect *jeune fille*.[1]

V

The kinds of rhythmic arrangement I have mentioned are not the most remarkable, but they are varied enough and also typical enough to lead already into the question—why do novelists resort to this kind of arrange-

[1]Conrad is an equally accomplished master of gradation. He is not mentioned here because I have nothing to add to what I have said of his mastery in "James and Conrad" (*Yale Review*, Winter, 1946).

ment? A simple answer was given by Zola when he was asked just after the appearance of the last in the Rougon-Macquart series why he had so often employed repetitive devices:

What you call repetitions occur in all my books. This is a literary device that I began by using with some timidity, but have since pushed perhaps to excess. In my view it gives more body to a work, and strengthens its unity. The device is somewhat akin to the motifs in Wagner, and if you will ask some musical friend of yours to explain his use of these, you will understand pretty well my use of the device in literature.

Undoubtedly repetitions make for unity. *The Ambassadors* is in E. M. Forster's view a triumph of pattern, that is of the imposition of a unifying order. And if Brooke of Tipton is forever saying the same things in the same words; if Esther Waters returns to let her life ebb where her life in the story began; if Jocelyn Pierston's great loves are all for the women of one family as they reach the same age; if the scorn the Baines sisters had in their youth for older people is turned against them in their age; if all Becky Sharp's revolutions in society leave her near the point where they began; if Goriot's daughters are revealed as indistinguishable in their egotism, and Harlov's as differing in the master trait of cruelty only in degree; if James's sensitive Americans in Paris respond to the same appeals, with only a variation in subtlety and intensity—one thing is certain, in all these renderings of life a unifying order has been imposed.

Zola was equally perceptive in saying that by repetitions a work might attain greater force, more body. While I was thinking about the effects of repetition I came on a pathetic passage in a letter by a novelist who is now completely forgotten. Mrs. Oliphant suffered many family griefs. A few years after her marriage her husband whose illness had driven the family to Rome died there of tuberculosis. When she felt she could bear to see Rome again, and again took her children there, her only daughter died after an illness of a few days. By a pen that must have been the most industrious in the Victorian age—it finally left a painful hole in her finger—she made a living for her sons, and for the children of her brother. When after about twenty years the pressure was abating a little, one of the sons was attacked by a congestion of the lungs. As she prepared to take him to the south of Europe which had twice been so fatal, the poor woman wrote to a friend:

> You know how anxiety of this kind acts upon me. I am in a suppressed fever, and can think of nothing else day and night. I watch every morsel he eats, every varying look and change of colour. How strange it is! All my troubles, and God knows they have been neither few nor small, have been repetitions—always one phase or another coming back, and that makes it all the worse, for I know how far my anguish can go.

What Mrs. Oliphant proved to herself in her life, we may prove in fiction. Repetition, expected and then presented, enforces the idea or the feeling, makes it more emphatic in its resonance. But in Mrs. Oliphant's life disaster never repeated itself exactly; the repetitive element was marked and dominant, but in each of the recurrences there was an important variation. Her husband and her daughter died in the same place, but not of the same disease, nor at the same pace. Her son was attacked by the same disease that had taken her husband; but she learned of her son's plight not on the Continent but at home. In fiction, also, the rhythmic arrangements that move us most are those like Thackeray's and Bennett's and James's where repetition is enveloped in variations, but never so enveloped that it appears subordinate.

When Zola compared his repetitive devices with Wagnerian motifs, he thought, I suppose, of effects that went beyond the strengthening of unity and the increase of force. Whether he did or not, I believe that a rhythmic arrangement can do more than unify and intensify. I shall try to explain what else it can do in the following discourses.

II

EXPANDING SYMBOLS

OR "the vagueness that afflicts all criticism of novels" one reason, I have said, is our inability to possess a novel as picture or a lyric can be possessed. Another is the inadequate vocabulary for describing the aspects of a novel —"most words provisional," as Virginia Woolf complained, "many metaphorical, and some on trial for the first time." "We have not," she says, "named and therefore presumably not recognized the simplest of devices by which every novel has to come into being."

The names given to the few aspects or devices that have been recognized come mainly from other kinds of literature and from other arts. Flaubert described *Madame Bovary* as a biography, "a biography rather than a developed perspective," yet the principle of a biography and the principle of a novel are quite unlike. The subject of a biography has no private thoughts or feelings. He consists solely of what he has done, said, written, and of the impressions and judgments formed by some of those who knew him. We do not know Scott as we know Jonathan Oldbuck or Dickens as we know Pecksniff or old Dorrit. Occasionally a novel is written within the limits of the biographical form, a novel in the form of a memoir like *The Way of All Flesh* or *The Late George Apley*. But the central character in a novel is generally a person whose abundant private thoughts and feelings are as well known to us as our own. "Nothing is unknown to writers of biographies of the present kind," Thackeray remarks at the beginning of *The Virginians*. Nothing about Emma Bovary that matters remains unknown; and a great many of the most telling pages in her story would not be conceivable if she were the subject of a pure biography. The use of such a term as "biography" to describe the kind of book in which she lives was a falling back on an approximation, a concession that even for Flaubert the *mot juste* was still to seek. If it is not a case of the language Virginia Woolf deplored, it is a case of language that was borrowed and, like most borrowed properties, does not fit.

In recent years novelists and critics have turned to arts outside literature to supplement the vocabulary for the description of prose fiction. More than anyone else Henry James has determined the vocabulary for modern English and American criticism of the genre. He believed at one time that there was "no essential difference between the painting of a picture and the writing of a novel"; and I doubt that he overcame this opinion. From the criticism of painting James took such terms as "values" and "lights," "foreshortening" and "perspective." His prefaces offer extraordinary combinations of these terms with others borrowed from drama. Since his *Portrait of a Lady*, how many novelists have used that word "portrait" in a title: Joyce's *Portrait of the Artist as a Young Man*, Sir Hugh Walpole's *Portrait of a Man with Red Hair*, Charles Morgan's *Portrait in a Mirror*. . . . Yet the difference between a novel and a portrait is essential. A portrait must fasten upon a single moment in the life of its subject; it is characteristic of a novel to linger over a score of moments, or even a

hundred. It seems natural enough to us that Willa
Cather should account for the structure of *The Professor's House* with its story within a story, by pointing
to the effect achieved by so many Dutch painters who
enrich the picture of an interior by a reflection in a
mirror of a street scene. Yet a novel must achieve its
effect in a fashion very different from any painting;
the story and the story within the story cannot be
apprehended simultaneously.

In our time music has been a resource as well as
painting. Titles such as Aldous Huxley's *Point Counter
Point,* Gide's *Symphonie pastorale,* Rumer Godden's *A
Fugue in Time,* no longer surprise us. It is to music that
E. M. Forster went for the term "rhythm" to express an
idea which will run through this discourse. I am sympathetic to Edwin Muir's complaint that "we do not
really believe that a novel has a pattern like a carpet
or a rhythm like a tune." I wish there were a term
peculiar to prose fiction for the set of devices that
Forster calls rhythmic. For the device I am interested
in exploring in this discourse the best specific term I
can fabricate is "expanding symbol."

II

The only examples of expanding symbols that Forster
mentions are from *A la recherche du temps perdu.*[1] He
elaborates but one of these symbols, the little phrase in
Vinteuil's music.

Vinteuil—Proust never gives him a Christian name—

[1] To the studies in Proust of my colleague Robert Vigneron I owe
much of the general framework of these pages, and am besides in-
debted to him for a number of particular ideas, but I must not hold
him responsible for the thesis.

was an obscure and unhappy organist and music teacher living in the depths of the French provinces. He appears in the novel only once, very early, a fussy, unsure, strait-laced citizen; and is later summed up as a solemn conventional little bourgeois. We should forget Vinteuil very quickly as just a trifling piece of the provincial *décor* like the *curé,* if his photograph were not desecrated in a scene of sadism in which his daughter engages with a Lesbian friend. We attend closely to this scene as Proust means we should. When his publisher asked him to leave it out as an unnecessary affront, he replied that although it led on to nothing in the first part of the novel, it was essential to the structure of the whole. If we attend to the scene, we do not much attend to the information imparted in the course of it that, besides giving lessons and playing the organ in the old church at Combray, Vinteuil composes. The tone that other persons in the novel take towards him suggests that anything he may compose would scarcely be worth hearing.

A hundred pages pass. Charles Swann, whose country house is near Vinteuil's town, attends a musical soirée in Paris. A year earlier at a similar party he had heard a sonata which had moved him beyond any other music; but all his efforts on that night and in the intervening months have not brought him the name of the work or its author, or a chance to hear it played again. Now he has a second chance. The sonata, and especially one recurrent little phrase, seems to Swann to hold the essence of his tragic jealous love for Odette. The little phrase in the sonata reaches a layer in his being never touched till now; it goes deeper even than his love. The sonata becomes the "national anthem" of the love between Swann and Odette; and every evening when they join the Verdurins and their party, the orchestra —Madame Verdurin is as inseparable from an orchestra as Sherlock Holmes from his pipe—strikes up the sonata. It is Vinteuil's.

Swann is not the only person for whom the sonata, and especially its little phrase, has a unique meaning. It is true that to the Verdurins and their guests the music has nothing to say: they cherish it only because it has a snob appeal. Odette is a stupid and insensitive woman, and Proust gives us no reason to suppose that she was less stupid or insensitive than usual in her response to the sonata, although she could play it charmingly. The sonata is like Herder's conception of God, compared by Goethe to a bowl which you will find empty unless you can put something in it. But some hundreds of pages after Swann has learned the secret of the authorship and after the work has been linked to his appearances in the world of the Verdurins and to his love for Odette, he plays the sonata for the narrator whom I shall call Marcel. And Marcel is also acutely and immediately affected. He puts more into the bowl than Swann could.

To him the sonata discloses, on repeated hearing, deeper and ever deeper levels of meaning. He quickly becomes dissatisfied with Swann's commentary on it, for Swann cannot detach the music from the vicissitudes of his love for Odette. In one of his struggles to articulate what the litle phrase means for him, Swann describes it as the Bois de Boulogne on a moonlit night fallen into a cataleptic trance; but this is merely because it was on such a night, to the music of Vinteuil, that Swann's love had known its happiest moment.

There is more than his love in Swann's response to the music, but what, he can never say. His failure to abstract from its material circumstances what had been most precious in his love, and to discover the link between that and the little phrase is an example of Swann's principal intellectual weakness—the inability he has inherited from his father to pursue a train of thought through any labyrinth of even moderate complexities.

Marcel has no such defect, far from it, and he may fairly be said to begin with the sonata almost where Swann leaves off. As a boy he too had known Vinteuil by sight; and he too had been scornful of the provincial organist. Unlike Swann he had come upon the crucial circumstance in Vinteuil's life: the inversion of his daughter. This had horrified Vinteuil, darkened his reading of life and brought him to a premature death. Marcel's approach to Vinteuil's music is clearer for the biographical knowledge; and since inversion becomes increasingly the sinister, horrifying element in the novel, what Vinteuil wrote seems to present an oblique and rewarding commentary on the theme, a commentary difficult to reduce to words, but perhaps all the more moving.

Long after Marcel has responded to the sonata, in *The Captive*—the sixth part of the novel—he attends a musical soirée at the Verdurins', a soirée that Swann cannot attend, for not only has he quarrelled with the Verdurins, he is dead. The first work played perplexes Marcel. It has a link with something in his past, and he wonders who can have composed it. Suddenly "the little phrase, more marvellous than any maiden, enveloped, harnessed with silver, glittering with brilliant effects of sound, as light and soft as silken scarves, came towards" him. This was no sonata; but a far more elaborate work, a septet, now played for the first time. The septet is a much deeper, and much more tragic, expression of Vinteuil than the sonata. It induces in Marcel reveries of threatening dawns, gradually giving way to the serenity of noon, sunny, almost rustic, with suggestions of the church square at Combray, Vinteuil's town, where Marcel had passed his vacations in childhood. The tribute to simple joys in the early part of the septet is, at first hearing, a disappointment to the sophisticated Marcel. But as the work moves towards its close, the disappointment is quieted; and once more attuned to the music of Vinteuil, Marcel reflects that this is the "masterpiece triumphant and complete." The interrogations are more urgent, and more perturbed than in the sonata; the responses more mysterious, more affecting. In the final movement, as Marcel's reveries evoke a stormy sunset, he attends to a phrase which had already figured in the sonata, but which had not acquired for him, in all the years he had known that work, the value he had perceived at once in the little phrase so cherished by Swann. In its new setting the long-neglected phrase becomes overwhelming; it is as splendid as some archangel of Mantegna's playing the trumpet. It is, Proust says elusively, "perhaps the only Stranger" Marcel ever had the fortune to meet.

What the septet means for Marcel is something more abstract than the meaning of the sonata for Swann. Vinteuil's music spoke to Swann of his love for Odette; it speaks now to Marcel of his love for Albertine. But to Marcel it speaks also of something that Swann did not, and could never, know: the essential meaning of art. It conveys to Marcel what a work of art should be, the kind of substance it should express, and the kind of form the expression should take. It conveys to him what Albertine and all the other elements in his painful life should mean for him in so far as he is an artist, and how that meaning might be transmuted into literature. It is his catalyst.

And how was the great septet, complete and triumphant, the last of Vinteuil's works, made available? In the dreadful days of his last year Vinteuil had been able merely to note it down in scrawls on scraps of paper. These seemed quite indecipherable. But Vinteuil's destroyer, his daughter's Lesbian friend, was also his saviour, the saviour at least of his music. She understood how his spirit moved, and the little ways of his pen, and where no one else could even surmise, she moved with absolute assurance. She had taken his daughter from him, but by rescuing his septet she was to give him immortality. It is a strange ambivalent relationship; and has a parallel in Marcel's love-affair with Albertine, on which as on so many other aspects of his development (and Proust's), the spirit and the fortune of Vinteuil offer a suggestive gloss.

Through the rest of the novel Vinteuil's music is seldom mentioned; but in the final part, two hundred pages before the end, Marcel once more insists on the difference between his understanding of that music and Swann's. It is a difference in depth: he understands all that Swann had understood; and he understands so much more. Vinteuil, he reminds us, was a great artist— he is the greatest artist to appear in the novel; there is something of his meaning that only another artist can catch. Even if Swann had lived to hear the septet he would not have found in it what Marcel found.

In *Marcel Proust, sa révélation psychologique,* Arnaud Dandieu declares that the first to point out the role Vinteuil's music has in the novel was E. M. Forster. Vinteuil's music was the subject of Benoist-Mechin's *La Musique et l'immortalité dans l'œuvre de Marcel Proust* (1926), but it was presented there in terms of emotional and philosophic meaning, not at all as a form of structure in the novel. Forster contrasts Proust's use of the music with another mode of using symbols in the novel: "Heard by various people—first by Swann, then by the hero—the phrase of Vinteuil is not tethered: it is not a banner such as we find George Meredith using—a double-blossomed cherry tree to accompany Clara Middleton, a yacht in smooth waters for Cecilia Halkett." I interrupt the quotation to protest that it is unjust to Meredith. He does use a luxurious yacht moving serenely along a harbour as a symbol for Cecilia, the daughter of its wealthy Tory owner. Nevil Beauchamp, looking back towards the yacht and the girl, sees in both images of "beautiful servicelessness." But this comparison is not to be taken as a unit in itself. Lord Palmet likens Jenny Denham, one of Cecilia's rivals with Beauchamp, a girl whose opinions are as radical as anyone could wish, to a "yacht before the wind." The two images illuminate and enrich each other. Moreover they are set, as is proper for *Beauchamp's Career,* centring in a naval officer, in a profusion of marine and nautical imagery and reference, from which they absorb added meaning.

For an instance of a fixed symbol, what Forster called

a "banner," I prefer to turn to *The Bridge of San Luis Rey*. That graceful and moving novel is arranged so that three times the same question is put, and three times the same answer is given. In the collapse of the bridge the five people crossing die. The question is whether the deaths were accidental disasters, instances of what Hardy called "crass casualty," or whether they were expressions of a design in the universe. Thornton Wilder first explores the lives of the Marquesa de Montemayor and her attendant, the girl Pepita. The lives of both were ruled by a great love, the Marquesa's for her daughter, Pepita's for the Abbess María del Pilar who had brought her up. Just before they travel to the bridge each has had an illumination—that her practice of love has been partly selfish—and each has already begun to act upon the discovery. Next is explored the life of the youth Esteban, whose great love has been for his identical twin, recently dead; Esteban too has had an illumination—that his grief for his twin has a selfish core—and has begun to act upon the discovery. The final exploration is into the life of Uncle Pio whose chief love has been for an actress who because of a horrible disfigurement will no longer see him. He too has just had an illumination—instead of repeating his efforts to see her, he has taken with her consent her son Jaime, and will bring him up as he had brought her up. Jaime is, it seems to me, a *ficelle*—his life is scarcely explored and need not be.

Each exploration confirms the others; but there is no reciprocal enrichment, no complication, subtilization, or expansion of meaning. For each of the travellers, except perhaps Jaime, the bridge is the same bridge. It is approached at the same spiritual moment, after regeneration, and for each the regeneration has been in the same terms of a reappraisal of love. The strongly repetitive nature of the symbol, by which it is fixed for us, is also revealed in the closing pages. Here persons the travellers have loved, and who know how different was the quality of the love just before the journey to the bridge, are shown to us, regenerated by the shock of the deaths and the revelation of the new levels of feeling scaled in the last days of the travellers' lives. "There is a land of the living and a land of the dead and the bridge is love, the only survival, the only meaning." That is the final sentence, a meditation by the wisest person in the novel, the Abbess María del Pilar. It tells nothing that we might not have known at the end of the first exploration. Unlike Proust's expanding symbols, the bridge accretes no new meanings, it has no fringe of unexhausted suggestions. Thornton Wilder's symbol, fixed and precise, *is* a banner that each of the travellers flies.

A banner [to return to Forster's commentary on Proust] can only reappear, rhythm can develop, and the little phrase has a life of its own, unconnected with the lives of its auditors, as with the life of the man who composed it. It is almost an actor, but not quite, and that "not quite" means that its power has gone towards stitching Proust's book together from the inside, and towards the establishment of beauty and the ravishing of the reader's memory. There are times when the little phrase—from its gloomy inception, through the sonata, into the sextet[1]—means everything to the reader. There are times when it means nothing and is forgotten, and this seems to me the function of rhythm in fiction; not to be there all the time like a pattern, but by its lovely waxing and waning to fill us with surprise and freshness and hope.

[1]In *Aspects of the Novel*, Forster calls the work a sextet. He corrects the slip in his paper "The Raison d'être of Criticism" in the Harvard symposium *Music and Criticism* (ed. R. F. French), although it still stands in recent reprintings of the earlier work.

This is not quite all that Forster says about Vinteuil's music, but the rest is preparation only. The stress upon the irregularity with which the symbol recurs is important, for the word rhythm at first suggests regularity, and without his pointing to irregularity as essential to beauty in the use of this kind of rhythm, we should have moved off in a false direction. No less important is his stress on Proust's giving a reader time to forget the music completely, for its last vibrations to subside and be as if they had never been. I am doubtful if Proust does achieve so complete a subsidence, or if he desired it. It is true that between the references to Vinteuil's music there are long distances but these tracts are broken by references to Vinteuil's nature, his shattered life, the abnormal actions and motives of his daughter and her unnamed friend, and the supposed improper intimacy between each of them and Marcel's Albertine, an intimacy about which most of Marcel's deepest anxieties gather. Many of these references, especially those in the earlier parts of the novel, are quite brief; but once we have felt, as Proust means us to feel, Swann's illumination, his irradiation, of spirit, in listening to Vinteuil's sonata, every reference to the composer's circumstances is a powerful reminder of what the music meant. I believe that if Proust's stitching is irregular it is much closer than Forster's statement suggests.

The observation that "the little phrase has a life of its own" is somewhat cryptic; but it is perhaps the most important of all Forster's claims for the expanding symbol. The effect that Proust achieves requires that Vinteuil's music should have different kinds of appeal

for the persons in his novel. I have said that for Madame
Verdurin and her coterie the music was simply a trophy
of snobbism, and that if Odette plays the sonata charmingly this is no reason for supposing that it has a profound meaning for her. Odette is an accomplished
courtesan, and she makes use of the sonata as she makes
use of mascara and pet names. Albertine's playing of
Vinteuil's music does not seem to have a deeper motive
than this. Only to Swann and to the narrator does the
music disclose a mysterious depth of meaning. Here,
as so often in the novel, Swann serves as preluding
character for Marcel, just as in *Point Counter Point*
Walter Bidlake serves as a preluding character for his
sister Elinor. "My love for Albertine," says Marcel, "had
repeated with important variations Swann's love for
Odette." The relation that links Swann's love and
Marcel's might have served as an example for the analysis in the preceding discourse of rhythmic arrangements of character. Marcel's response to Vinteuil's music
repeats with important variations Swann's response, in-
cluding and transcending it. That only two persons in
a novel with a huge cast of characters reach out towards
the mystery in the music, and that the second of these
two comes much nearer to it than the first, indicates
the depth of the symbol. I believe that Proust is inviting us to speculate whether even the narrator has
plucked the heart out of the symbol, whether there is
not a surplus of meaning in it to be disengaged only by
a yet more sensitive auditor, a yet more powerful
creative spirit. This is an observation that Forster does
not explicitly make; but I think that when he says that
the little phrase has a life of its own this is part of what

he is implying. Only if the symbol is given a surplus of meaning, can it continue to live the length of the novel, and to hold a reader's sense of its inexhaustible beauty.

Forster is so perceptive an interpreter of Vinteuil's music because he had used the expanding symbol before Proust did, and was to use it again, as a most important device towards the total effect of a novel.

Howards End is a study in personal relations. This sounds utterly commonplace; more than half of the memorable novels of our time hinge on personal relations. But Forster's concern with them is of a peculiar sort: indeed he often sets the phrase off by the marks of quotation. The question he is putting to us is whether his people can really have a personal relation. Cecil Vyse in *A Room with a View* "is the sort who are all right so long as they keep to things—books, pictures— but kill when they come to people." "He should know no one intimately. . . ." It is intended as a hopeless disqualification. At the beginning of another early novel, *The Longest Journey,* a girl appears in a gathering at a Cambridge college, and, after she has left, one boy asks another why he did not show her common politeness. The boy reproached answers that the girl was not really there. One cannot have a personal relation with someone who is not there. A great number of the persons in *Howards End* either are not really there, or are there so dimly and so feebly that a relation with them is not worth having if indeed it is possible at all. At the other end of the scale are persons who are intensely there for us, as for themselves, but Forster puts the question whether they are there for one another.

Where Proust depends on the complex morbid music of Vinteuil, Forster depends on hay. Hay is not the only expanding symbol in *Howards End,* but it is the most finely used. Hay rules the first pages of the novel, a letter to Margaret Schlegel from her sister, Helen, who is staying with the Wilcox family at their house in Hertfordshire, Howards End. Helen describes Ruth Wilcox, a Howard before she married, as moving through her garden, smelling a handful of hay, her dress trailing in the grass; and Ruth's husband and children, all victims of hay fever, as sneezing the moment that in their cult of fitness they venture outside. That Ruth Wilcox is beautifully at ease in the countryside and that she is unlike the rest of her family in this, is perhaps all the first chapter tells about the Wilcoxes. Very soon Ruth has a crisis to meet on the doorstep of Howards End, a crisis in personal relations, insults flying, mean assumptions forming; and she approaches "trailing noiselessly over the lawn, and there was actually a wisp of hay in her hands." "She seemed," says the novelist, in a passage that everyone who writes about him is eager to quote, "to belong not to the young people and their motor, but to the house, and to the tree that overshadowed it. One knew that she worshipped the past, and that the instinctive wisdom the past can alone bestow had descended upon her. . . ." Through her it descends upon the situation, and she is the easy mistress of the disagreeable crisis. Once it is over she stoops to smell a flower. The wisp of hay trailing in her hand, related now to the past as well as to the countryside, is as much part of the portrait of Ruth as the bow in the hand of Raphael's Apollo.

Early in the novel Ruth dies. A few years later her millionaire capitalist husband, an alien to the countryside and to the past, whose concern is with organizations, committees, things, and never with persons, marries Margaret Schlegel. Margaret is extraordinarily unlike Ruth: she has not a root in the countryside; she is stridently contemporary in her moods, and in her interests, which are artistic and intellectual. But Margaret and Ruth were drawn to each other: they existed for each other; they were persons and could have a personal relation. Ruth asked that Margaret Schlegel should have Howards End, it was her last request; but the request was disregarded by the Wilcoxes, and Howards End was shut up. Years and chapters have passed since we saw Ruth in her garden, before Mr. Wilcox takes Margaret for her first view of the house. While he goes for the keys, Margaret waits alone on the flagged porch before an apparently locked door, idly gathering not hay but some weeds that have pushed up between the flags. As she presses on the door, it springs open and, clutching the weeds, she enters. She is met by Miss Avery, a very old woman, who would have made an ideal companion for Miss Havisham in *Great Expectations,* a friend of Ruth, and caretaker of the house. "The old woman . . . said dryly, 'Oh! Well, I took you for Ruth Wilcox.' Margaret stammered: 'I—Mrs. Wilcox—?' 'In fancy, of course, in fancy. You had her way of walking.' " Margaret's bunch was of weeds, and she clutched it instead of trailing it. But Ruth had shown Margaret that a place can mean more than a person and had felt Margaret's response to this revelation. Ruth still seems to Margaret to have lived at the height of an incline that she does not have the power to mount; but the clutch at the weeds suggests that she has more than begun.

In the first crisis in her relations with Mr. Wilcox, the

discovery that years before he had had an awful mistress, Margaret talks with him in a garden. As she thinks of his first wife she bends over a mower and unconsciously lets grass trickle through her fingers. Relating herself to him though he cannot relate himself to her, she lets him off very lightly, as Ruth had always done; and crossing the hall to the stairs leaves a long trickle of grass on the floor. It is much the same with the last crisis in Margaret's relations with Mr. Wilcox. They are married and at odds about Helen. Margaret will not enter a Wilcox house; she suggests that her husband talk with her on a strip of grass that rises into the Six Hills, queer unexplained mounds supposed by Margaret to cover the graves of soldiers. As they talk, with the keys to Howards End lying beside them in the sunlight, Margaret's fingers drive unconsciously through the grass, and at the height of the conversation she seems to feel the Six Hills stirring. This is the moment of her victory. By it Mr. Wilcox grows—he does not grow much, it is late for him to grow at all, but he does grow—and the great final scenes would have been impossible if he had not.

The final scenes are more variously suggestive. Margaret has been married for some time, and living with Mr. Wilcox at Howards End. Helen is with her, and Helen's illegitimate son. The child's great-grandfather had been an agricultural labourer; but the London which is the capital of Wilcoxism had beckoned to the intermediate generations and reduced them from the sturdy farmer to the almost subhuman. At the end of the novel it is summer, as it had been in the beginning. Once more hay is everywhere. Margaret sits with her sister, with whom her personal

relations are beautifully true, on the edge of the
meadow where the hay is being cut. The baby tumbles
in the hay. Helen takes up a wisp, withered now, but,
as Margaret says, "it will sweeten tomorrow." Meanwhile Mr. Wilcox and his clan are holding council in
the dark and airless room to which their allergy confines them all. "There's not one Wilcox can stand up
against a field in June," as old Miss Avery has said,
with senile but delightful malice. Mr. Wilcox, who, in
his new phase, has decided that living at Howards
End is worth the discomfort, sends for Margaret and
announces that at his death his business, his stocks and
his bonds, all the apparatus of Wilcoxism, shall go to
the clan, but Howards End shall not—it shall go to
Margaret, and upon her death to the little boy whom
we left tumbling in the hay, and whom, with a shadow
of distaste, he calls his wife's er-r-r- nephew. Ruth's
intention is fulfilled through the power Margaret has
absorbed from her, and more than fulfilled, for Howards
End is saved from Wilcoxism not for one but for two
generations. With a characteristically impulsive movement Helen bursts into the airless room exclaiming, in
the last words of the novel, "The field's cut!—the big
meadow! We've seen to the very end, and it'll be such
a crop of hay as never." The Wilcoxes are reprieved,
soon they can go outside again; but the hay combines
with Ruth Howard's wish, and Margaret Schlegel's
personal relation with Mr. Wilcox, to convince them
that they are only temporary visitants at Howards End.

The sequence of the wisps of hay, the bunch of
weeds, the trickling grass, the grass on the Six Hills,
the bumper crop of hay, is not the only symbol for the
life that is immune to Wilcoxism. Forster makes use
also of the beautiful but unproductive vine that winds

along a wall—of course the Wilcoxes wanted it cut down; and also, more mysteriously, of a centenarian wych-elm, surely one of the most beautiful trees in literature. But from the hay and the other simple forms that are grouped with it, we can discover Forster's attachment to the expanding symbol. Before he has done with it, the hay is linked with everything that stands out against Wilcoxism: with the countryside and the past; with Margaret's cultivation of personal relations; with Helen's reckless revolt against the empire of business and convention; and, in the scarcely individuated baby, with a junction of the poor, the urban poor who have rural roots, and those generous elements in other classes which, if dependent on big business, are not defiled, depersonalized, by it. Above all these describable things stands, as presiding goddess, Ruth Howard, in whom there is something that no 'description can exhaust, any more than it can exhaust the hay itself.

Proust's use of the expanding symbol and Forster's are alike in more than the residue of mystery. Like the little phrase the hay has meaning only for a few of the characters; response to the hay, like response to the little phrase, is an index to value in a character. Proust withheld until rather late in the novel the response of the person for whom the little phrase had the greatest importance; but Forster sets Ruth Howard at the very beginning. The difference is less than appears; for if Ruth responds most intimately to the hay, she is incapable of expressing even to herself anything of why it is precious to her. In her aversion from analysis, she is another Charles Swann. The intellectual limitation combined in Ruth and in Swann with fine perceptiveness makes them the appropriate characters to offer the first deep response to an expanding symbol; and it is best for the expansion of the symbol that these two characters should die before the novel approaches its end. Margaret and Marcel, coming after Ruth and Swann, and having a gift for analysis and a delight in it, enable us to penetrate to qualities in the response of Ruth and Swann that otherwise we should surely have missed. They do this as well as penetrate to qualities in the expanding symbol that had either eluded (as with Swann), or touched only in mystical fashion (as with Ruth), the earlier characters.

The music of Vinteuil has far less to do with Proust's plot than the hay has to do with Forster's. The disposal of Howards End is essential to Forster's story—one hesitates to call it a plot: no less essential than the whale's destruction of Ahab, his crew, and his ship at the close of *Moby Dick*.[1] What Forster em-

---

[1] The white whale is an expanding symbol, the most impressive I have found in earlier fiction. Ahab finds far more meaning in the whale than anyone else does; and Ahab's insight grows as his spirit becomes ever more preoccupied with the whale. Yet when the whale at last appears, his intelligence and malice far outrun a reader's expectations. The whale has a life of his own, and of him may also be said what Melville says of his great antagonist: "As touching all Ahab's deeper part, every revelation partook more of significant darkness than of explanatory light." But Melville's use of the white whale has an unrelenting insistence: from the early chapters to the end the whale dominates the story, with no real subsidence. Nearer to Proust's use of Vinteuil's music and Forster's use of hay is the symbol of the coffin, associated with the whale. In the second chapter Ishmael lodges in New Bedford at the Spouter Inn, kept by Peter Coffin, and reflects: "Coffin?—Spouter?—Rather ominous in that particular connexion." In the epilogue Ishmael, the sole survivor, clings to the "coffin lifebuoy," made long before to please Queequeg. The recurrence of the coffin, with deepening but never fully explicit suggestion, through the novel, is comparable in method with Forster's expanding symbols.

bodies in the violent movement of the story towards its quiet and satisfying conclusion, he diffuses through the expanding symbol as a complementary expression of his meaning. The music of Vinteuil has a more shadowy relation to Proust's story. Like Bergotte's prose and Elstir's painting, it helps the narrator to define the place of art among the occupations of man and to decide that the practice of art is on the whole the best expression of human powers; and it also offers a mysterious clue to the role that evil can have in the realization of a good.

Howards End was in print a year before the manuscript of *Swann's Way* was ready for a publisher to see. In at least one of the earlier Forster novels, *The Longest Journey*, expanding symbols are used with great power and beauty although, I think, with less effect than in *Howards End*. The symbols in *A Room with a View* seem to me recurrent rather than expanding. From their number and the frequency with which they recur the background takes on an importance that often reduces the characters to dwarfs. The central symbol of the "view" is kept almost unrelentingly before us; but its full content is soon communicated, and the recurrence of the symbol is rather a reminder than a development. The interplay of light and darkness, almost as unrelenting, has an element of mystery that is never quite resolved, and so has the more finely and sparingly used symbol of water. It is in the use of water—from the Arno and back to the Arno, by way of rainstorms, and the Sacred Lake at Windy Corner, and the immaterial waves that beat in people's hearts and brains—that *A Room with a View* achieves the expansion of a symbol comparable with the hay in

Howards End. But it is almost impossible that Forster's usage should have affected Proust, who never mentions anything of Forster's, and read English—the only language in which any of Forster's novels could then be read—with extreme difficulty. I do not think there is much illumination for the practice of either novelist in inquiring what may have given him the notion of using the expanding symbol. But I shall hazard an opinion. I am almost certain that the device was suggested by musical works, and especially by Wagner's.

Forster has confessed that during the greater part of a performance of music he does not attend: he allows the sounds to send him woolgathering. This is what happens to Helen Schlegel when she hears the Fifth Symphony in an early chapter of *Howards End.* That afternoon in the Queen's Hall—since destroyed, as I have heard Forster comment, by the composer's countrymen—there was a rather large party. Margaret Schlegel heard only the music; Tibby, the girls' brother and a disciple of Cecil Vyse, watched for counterpoint, the score across his knees; their aunt waited for a tune so she might tap; their cousin Fräulein Mosebach could only remember that Beethoven was *echt Deutsch*; Fräulein Mosebach's young man could only remember that he was with Fräulein Mosebach. It is the woolgatherer Helen who is the author's counterpart; it is her response that he follows, and none of the others. For Helen there are goblins and elephants in the symphony; the goblins sneer at beauty and other values and the elephants trample on them; but the elephants pause and are still, and heroes eject the goblins; despite the magnificent affirmations of the heroes, the goblins return. Once more they are ejected; but they could return again, and again, and again. "He had said so bravely, and that is why one can trust Beethoven when he says other things."

Marcel listened to music as Helen did, to Vinteuil's and to Wagner's, from which a part of Vinteuil's descended. Marcel hears the laughter of Siegfried, immortally young, and the great blows of the hero's hammer. Forster drew the same kind of pleasure from listening to Wagner. "I used," he wrote a few years ago, "to be very fond of music that reminded me of something and especially fond of Wagner. With Wagner I always knew where I was—he ordained that one phrase should recall the ring, another the sword, another the blameless fool, and so on; he was as precise in his indications as an Oriental dancer."

But the source of the device is of merely curious interest. Proust claims he found much the same sort of pleasure in the structure of Ruskin's thought in the lectures collected as *Sesame and Lilies*. The suggestion is at first startling; but any one who knows Ruskin's massively varied and yet intensely repetitive art in prose will see what it means. What matters is not the source, or even the kind of source, but the function and effect of the device.

The expanding symbol is of special use when the idea or feeling the novelist is rendering is subtle or otherwise elusive. To the novelist whose reading of life is clear and convinced it cannot be an appropriate tool. It would not serve Anthony Trollope's purposes. He is visited by no doubts as to what went on in Barsetshire; he is secure in his conviction that he knows every last fold in the consciousness of Mrs. Proudie, her bishop, and her retainers, of Eleanor Bold and the Signora

Vesey-Neroni. There is nothing in them that resists clear and convinced expression, except for the episcopal chaplain's rather coarse passion for Eleanor and the central element in the Signora's welcome to any half-promising male. Trollope could express these matters with perfect clarity and conviction if he were not sensitive to the tabus of the circulating library, and alarmed by the power of fiction to demoralize the virtuous young. Apart from this one restriction Trollope can render his entire meaning and never resort to anything beyond the conventional elements in the structure of the novel—story, people, place, and comment.

To a writer who is not so confident that life is perfectly intelligible, and who is impelled to render the part of life that eludes his clear and convinced understanding, the symbol, fixed or expanding, is a chief resource. "In a Symbol," Carlyle said, "there is concealment and yet revelation; here, therefore, by Silence and by Speech acting together, comes a double significance." The fixed symbol, Thornton Wilder's bridge, or E. M. Forster's "view," has but little concealment: it is very close to explicit statement. There is a powerful case of the fixed symbol in *War and Peace*. Pierre Bezukhov, falling in love with Natasha Rostov, looks up into the sky to see the great comet of 1812. The association between the sight and the emotion is lasting; it adds to our feeling how strong, and how remarkable, his love is—but does it have the least bit of mysterious implication of which Forster's references to Orion in *The Longest Journey* are all compact?

The expanding symbol is a device far more appropriate for rendering an emotion, an idea, that by its largeness or its subtlety cannot become wholly explicit.

The fixed symbol is almost entirely repetition; the expanding symbol is repetition balanced by variation, and that variation is in progressively deepening disclosure. By the slow uneven way in which it accretes meaning from the succession of contexts in which it occurs; by the mysterious life of its own it takes on and supports; by the part of its meaning that even on the last page of the novel it appears still to withhold—the expanding symbol responds to the impulses of the novelist who is aware that he cannot give us the core of his meaning, but strains to reveal now this aspect of it, now that aspect, in a sequence of sudden flashes.

The expanding symbol serves the novelist who is, to take a term from the *Aspects of the Novel*, "prophetic." A novelist of the prophetic kind differs from his brothers in that he intends not to say anything, but to "sing in the halls of fiction." "The strangeness of song arising in the halls of fiction," E. M. Forster admits, "is bound to give us a shock." Many readers find the shock so disagreeable that they would have the singer desist—and put his song into a more appropriate medium. The particular idea or emotion that impels the novelist to sing, the belief that Emily Brontë held about the extension of the individual personality beyond the bounds of the self ("I am Heathcliff")—the belief that E. M. Forster holds about a redemptive personal relation ("You and I and Henry are only fragments of that woman's mind") —the belief that D. H. Lawrence held about the unconscious, is not the most important thing: what is most important is that the idea or feeling requires from the novelist the bardic tone. The prophetic novelist is struggling—with him there is always a struggle —to communicate an emotion about something that lies behind his story and his people and his setting, about something much more general, much less definite than any of these. What Forster says of Dostoevski will perhaps make this inherently obscure something a trifle less obscure. I have found it an illustration that really illumines:

> In Dostoevsky the characters and situations always stand for more than themselves; infinity attends them, though they remain individuals they expand to embrace it and summon it to embrace them. . . . Every sentence he writes implies this extension, and the implication is the dominant aspect of his work. He is a great novelist in the ordinary sense—that is to say his characters have relation to ordinary life and also live in their own surroundings, there are incidents which keep us excited and so on; he has also the greatness of a prophet, to which our ordinary standards are inapplicable.

Now if the novelist needs to direct us to something behind the story, the people, and the setting; if the story, the people, and the setting are to be infused by something greater than they, the expanding symbol may help. It warns the reader that he must look beyond the foreground where he can safely keep his eyes in a novel by Trollope or Thackeray. Dostoevski takes us beyond the fuss over the murder of the elder Karamazov, beyond the loves and ambitions of the Karamazov brothers, beyond Russia. He does not do it by the expanding symbol; but it is by the expanding symbol that Proust and Forster take us beyond their story, their persons, their settings.

One remark more, of a somewhat speculative kind. Rhythm is an order. For all its elusiveness the expanding symbol in its rhythmic evolution is a form of order; no matter how far the symbol expands, the music of Vinteuil, or the hay in *Howards End*, has a constant nucleus. By the use of an expanding symbol, the novelist persuades and impels his readers towards two beliefs. First, that beyond the verge of what he can express, there is an area which can be glimpsed, never surveyed. Second, that this area has an order of its own which we should greatly care to know—it is neither a chaos, nor something irrelevant to the clearly expressed story, persons, and settings that fill the foreground. The glimpses that are all the novelist can give us of this area do not suffice for our understanding how it is ordered, they merely assure us that it is ordered, and that this order is important to us. The use of the expanding symbol is an expression of belief in things hoped for, an index if not an evidence of things not seen. It does not say what these things are like: it sings of their existence. To fall back on the words Elizabeth Brentano ascribed to Beethoven, by the expanding symbol we are permitted "an incorporeal entrance into the higher world of knowledge which comprehends mankind, but which mankind cannot comprehend."

III

INTERWEAVING THEMES

OR ONE of the devices called rhythmical by E. M. Forster I preferred a specific term—the *expanding symbol*. Forster extends the meaning of rhythm to include another device, quite unlike the expanding symbol, although it too depends on repetition with variation and it too serves the novelist who would sing in the halls of fiction and invite the reader to attend to the knowledge which comprehends mankind but which mankind cannot comprehend. The specific term I shall use for this kind of rhythm is an *interweaving theme*. What Forster says about his second kind of rhythm, the "difficult rhythm," as he calls it, is brief and elusive. I may not fully understand it, but what part of it I do understand has enabled me to read a number of novels with an increase of pleasure and insight.

This kind of rhythm depends, Forster says, mainly but not entirely on a relationship between the larger parts of a novel analogous to the relationship between the movements in a sonata or a symphony. Forster professes himself unable to cite an example of this kind of rhythm in prose fiction. "The other rhythm," he says, "the difficult one—the rhythm of the Fifth Symphony as a whole —I cannot quote you any parallels for that in fiction, yet it may be present." I do not believe that this teasing remark means just what it at first appears to mean. I believe that E. M. Forster had clearly in his mind a superb example of interweaving themes in fiction, and that modesty alone prevented him from naming it. Throughout the *Aspects of the Novel* he never refers to his own practice of fiction. About *A Passage to India* as an example of themes beautifully interwoven I shall have something to say in the next discourse.

At the very end of his few suggestive paragraphs on the difficult kind of rhythm, E. M. Forster does mention, hesitantly, reluctantly, a novel in which he thinks it may exist—*War and Peace*. In *War and Peace*, he writes in the essay on Proust, published two years after the *Aspects*, there is "a rhythmic rise-fall-rise of the generations"; and in the *Aspects*, less precisely, he says of the effect of rhythm as achieved in *War and Peace* that it is like the hearing, when the novel has been read and laid aside, of great chords sounding behind us, every item in the book, even to the catalogue of strategies, "leading a larger existence than was possible at the time" when it lay before us on the page.

In the Rede lecture on Virginia Woolf, E. M. Forster remarks: "*To the Lighthouse* is in three movements. It has been called a novel in sonata form." *To the Lighthouse* came out only in the same year that Forster gave the lectures published as *Aspects of the Novel*. Whether he had read it before he wrote his lectures, he tells me he cannot now, after a lapse of over twenty years, recall; but among Virginia Woolf's novels it has remained his favourite.

To the Lighthouse, so much less complicated than Tolstoy's book, brief and bare by comparison, will perhaps show more readily what is meant by the rhythmic relationship between the parts of a prose fiction. The three books into which the novel is explicitly divided are called "The Window," "Time Passes," and "The Lighthouse." In the first of these we witness, mainly through the eyes of a very young painter, Lily Briscoe, the passage of an afternoon and evening at the Ramsays' cottage in the Hebrides. The brief second book traces an interval of many years during which Mrs. Ramsay and two of her children die, and the cottage lies empty and decaying. In the third book, we witness, again mainly through the eyes of Lily Briscoe, a morning at the cottage when Mr. Ramsay and the two youngest children make the long-intended voyage to the lighthouse. Mr. Bernard Blackstone in his recent commentary on Virginia Woolf has labelled the three parts "integration," "disintegration," and "reintegration." The words may be repulsive, and a professor on this side of the Atlantic would be laughed at in the English weeklies for proposing them; but the idea is sound, and the words themselves are helpful when one is approaching *To the Lighthouse* with a musical analogy in mind.

The dominant theme in the first book is the splendour of life. But there is much in that book at war with this theme. Mr. Ramsay, a distinguished metaphysician, had written at twenty-five a book of real importance; then he married for love, and had eight children; and what he had written since his marriage was also repetition and amplification. Wife and large family were necessary to him—he could not be secure without them; but had they not clipped his wings? At least the wings will not bear him where he wants to go. Lily Briscoe cannot paint as she would like to paint. At the cottage she is trying again: on the lawn she is painting the cottage, with, at the centre of the picture, Mrs. Ramsay, dressed in white, sitting at the window. Lily cannot render what she sees. It is the same with the other members of the large vacation party. This one is edgy, another melancholy, a third cold, and none resiliently happy, at ease, at one with the group. The voyage to the lighthouse that Mrs. Ramsay is to take the next day with her youngest son James is involved in petty bickering with her husband. The part ends before the next day comes, the voyage resting in doubt, probably not to be made.

But the splendour of life is nevertheless the dominant theme of the part. It is rendered in terms of food, love, and society, and the greatest of these is society. The central scene is at dinner. The *bœuf-en-daube* becomes poetic by the delicacy and sensuous devotion in Virginia Woolf's way of celebrating its look, its savour, and its taste. Love has its part at the table: the handsomest young man and the prettiest girl in the company arrive late because they have become engaged that afternoon, and the radiance of Minta Doyle vies with the glory of the *bœuf-en-daube*. But the dinner is most of all a triumph not of food or of love, but of what I have far too prosaically called society. Some of the people at the table are unattractive individuals—Charles Tansley, although there is no harm in him, is surely one of the most unamiable persons in fiction; it would be less painful to have dinner with Anna Karenina's husband and listen to the cracking of his finger-joints. Mrs. Ramsay's special power, appreciated by her guests, is in the fusion of the chance-collected, discordant, even recalcitrant individuals. Out of three ordinary sounds Browning's musician made not a fourth sound but a star, and out of her unpromising miscellany Mrs. Ramsay makes a communion. There is singing in the

halls of fiction. Literally so. Mr. Ramsay repeats the
lines:

> Come out and climb the garden path,
>   Luriana, Lurilee.
> The China rose is all abloom and buzzing with the yellow bee

and as the recitation continues, Mrs. Ramsay feels as if
what her husband was declaiming were what her own
voice might have been uttering, and she knows, without
having to glance about, that all the miscellaneous
company shares her sense that one was speaking for all.
As she rose to leave the room, the dinner over, the poet
Augustus Carmichael (a touching and beautiful portrait,
to whom no critic of the novel has done even half
justice) rose too, and where Mr. Ramsay had merely
spoken, chants the lines:

> To see the Kings go riding by
> Over lawn and daisy lea
> With their palm leaves and cedar sheaves,
>   Luriana, Lurilee.

As Mrs. Ramsay passed him Augustus Carmichael
turned but very slightly towards her and repeated:

> Luriana, Lurilee.

As he bowed to her, "without knowing why, she felt
that he liked her better than he had ever done before;
and with a feeling of relief and gratitude she returned
his bow and passed through the door which he held
open for her."

Literal singing, and singing that is of the sort E. M.
Forster found in *Wuthering Heights,* and in *The
Brothers Karamazov.* The splendour of life is hymned
in a fashion that takes us from the foreground, from the

quiet little fable, the gentle estimable characters, to the infinities that attend them.

The second book is sombre and full of lamentation. Until very late it has nothing to say about the splendour of life. It is concerned with decay, waste, death. Mrs. Ramsay dies in a parenthesis; and two of her children die almost as briefly. The cottage decays and for years no one enters it. The place of union, of splendid life, has become the place of death. But as this painful middle movement of the novel is about to end, the theme of decay, waste, death is challenged, is suddenly, and strongly, interrupted and opposed. The cottage is got ready for the return of the Ramsays after years of absence. Decay is arrested by the gardeners and cleaning women—themselves ageing, aching, decaying; waste is over; the potentiality of life in the cottage proves tough, too tough for all the varied forms in which death has assailed it.

In the third book they go to the lighthouse. It is Mr. Ramsay who insists; his son James, so eager to go in the first book, did not (we learn) make the voyage with his mother the morning after that book ended, and now James starts out sulkily. They are going, Mr. Ramsay, James, and the daughter Cam, because in the first book Mrs. Ramsay had meant to go, wanted to go; and Mr. Ramsay had been captious, quarrelsome, difficult, and no one had gone. To Mr. Ramsay the voyage is the payment of an intimate debt. And what wonderful consequences flow from the voyage! A union is established as at the dinner in the first book. The union includes those who do not go to the lighthouse as well as those who do. Lily Briscoe is on the lawn as she was in the afternoon described in the first part; and again she is painting the cottage. As the little boat approaches the lighthouse, Lily seems to see Mrs. Ramsay's white dress fluttering in its proper place by the window, and she knows precisely how she is to complete her painting. Augustus Carmichael lies beside her on the lawn. Lily rises as Mrs. Ramsay had risen at the end of the dinner; and Augustus Carmichael rises as he had risen then. Both look out to sea. Mr. Ramsay is on more intimate terms with his son and daughter than he has ever been; and Lily and Augustus Carmichael are at one with each other and with those in the boat, especially with Mr. Ramsay. "Reintegration" is Mr. Blackstone's word: not only has decay been arrested and the cottage regained for life; not only has death been routed, for Mrs. Ramsay's power to make a union among the miscellaneous and discordant persists beyond her own personal life. More than this may be said: this union will endure longer than the union at the dinner which Mrs. Ramsay knew would begin to disintegrate the moment she left the room and all scattered to their peculiar concerns.

The theme interwoven with the singing of the splendour of life is heard again in the final part of the novel, but less strongly, less often. In the middle part it rose to its height of emphasis, it almost prevailed. Now the splendour prevails, and suspicion, sulkiness, fear, and melancholy recede before it.

As we lay the book down undoubtedly we may hear those great chords of which E. M. Forster spoke. Undoubtedly every item in the book, even Mrs. Ramsay's darning, now leads for us a larger existence than was possible when we first knew of it. The three parts of the novel are related somewhat as the three big blocks of sound in a sonata. Must we be content with such an approximation? E. M. Forster is amusing about attempts to find in one art what is found in another. "When music reminded me of something which was not music, I supposed it was getting me somewhere. 'How like Monet!' I thought when listening to Debussy, and 'how like Debussy!' when looking at Monet. I translated sounds into colours, saw the piccolo as apple green and the trumpets as scarlet. The arts were to be enriched by taking in one another's washing." At least I may say that in the interweaving of themes as in the management of gradation in character and incident, the novelist is achieving his effect by repetition modified by variation, and thus link what Virginia Woolf has done not only with music but with other resources in the art of fiction.

II

From *To the Lighthouse* it would be an easy step to a novel of Forster's which nearly resembles it, the most purely beautiful of his books, although the least appreciated since it is the most puzzling. But *The Longest Journey*, just because the interweaving in it of integration, disintegration, reintegration is so complex, will not help as an illustration. Because of the complexity of interweaving I must also avoid anything of Thomas Mann's, and there is another reason for avoiding both *The Magic Mountain* and the much more delicate *Death in Venice*, the most perfect of his works—in his conduct of themes as in his conduct of expanding symbols there is a geometrical precision by which some of the most precious effects these devices can achieve are quite precluded. Instead I pass to a simpler novel, Willa Cather's *The Professor's House,* which came out two years before Forster gave his lectures on the art of the novel.

Willa Cather's fiction unlike Virginia Woolf's preserves most of the conventional elements; but in her writing there is a steadily growing concern with what is too subtle or too large to be wholly fixed in a story, or in people, or even in setting, a concern with what calls for the hovering of suggestion rather than for bold and outright statement. Even in her early novels, in *O Pioneers!, My Antonia, The Song of the Lark,* there was something neither story nor persons nor places, something felt by those who feel it at all as a large background of emotion. As she grew older the large background of emotion claimed more and more of her attention; and by its demands the structure of her novels underwent very interesting and beautiful change. The change is apparent in *The Professor's House,* although the triumphant use of the new structure is in the subsequent *Death Comes for the Archbishop,* which she wisely judged her finest book. In *The Professor's House,* there is energetic narrative, there are memorable people, and there is a strong and yet delicate realization of setting. You may read the book for any of these, or for all three, but you will not be reading the novel that Willa Cather wrote unless you find something else. There is an astonishing comment on *The Professor's House* in Alexander Porterfield's essay on Willa Cather, the most considered English estimate of her novels. Mr. Porterfield says: "Briefly, it is the story of a scholarly professor at a Middle Western university, passing through the critical uneasy period between middle and old age—at least it should be taken as a study of such, otherwise its meaning is difficult to perceive exactly." Well, its meaning is difficult to perceive exactly, but I am startled to find a critic shutting the door on his perception that there is more in a book than he can quite apprehend, and shaking himself, and deciding that his apprehension is the measure of the novelist's meaning.

The Professor's House has been a perplexity to most critics. For my part I believe that it is by scrutinizing the author's approach to houses that we may best discover the extraordinary relation between the three parts into which, like *To the Lighthouse,* it is explicitly divided.

At the outset Willa Cather presents Professor Godfrey St. Peter living between two houses. There is the expensive conventional new house that he has built because his wife wanted it, and into which he has moved with reluctance, with a positive distaste that greatly surprises him; and there is the old rented frame house, ugly, inconvenient, run down, in which he has lived for thirty years—for the whole of his adult life, the whole of his career, the whole of his marriage. He finds that he can write, and think, only in its attic study, encumbered with the forms on which a dressmaker has fitted clothes for his wife and daughters ever since he was a young husband. It is oil-lit, and stove-heated; it has almost every disadvantage a room can have; but it has been the house of his mind and spirit. It is very easy to mark the two houses as symbols, of no mysterious depth. Nor do they acquire in the first part of the novel any depth beyond the practice of a Sinclair Lewis or a James Farrell.

The obviously startling element in the structure of *The Professor's House* is its second part, a long story inserted after the fashion of Cervantes or Smollett. The length, vitality, and power of the intercalated tale are startling, and not only at a first reading. The substance in this middle part of the novel is the crucial episode in the life of Tom Outland. Once and once only in the thirty years of his teaching, St. Peter had encountered a mind and personality of the first order, a student from whom he learned, and whose impress is strong upon the many-volumed history of Spanish exploration in America which brought St. Peter his fame, gave him his full mental and personal growth, and as a by-product provided the new house, built with literary prize money. When the novel opens Tom Outland is dead, killed, like one of the Ramsay sons, in the First World War.

The central event in Tom Outland's life was the discovery of a Cliff Dweller village in a New Mexican canyon. That discovery gave a new dimension to American life for Outland and later for St. Peter. Here was beauty, the beauty of pure and noble design, unspoiled by clutter or ornament, undistracted by cosiness, uncontradicted by the ugliness of machinery and industry. An expert to whom Tom showed some of the pottery was struck by its likeness to the decorative art of early Crete, and in this suggestion there is nothing fantastic. The effect Willa Cather produces in her account of the Cliff Dwellers is very near Keats's evocation of the Greek town in the "Ode on a Grecian Urn." The houses of the Cliff Dwellers are never overtly contrasted with those in the Middle Western university town where the first and third parts of the novel are laid; and in the modern town the emphasis falls upon individual buildings, in the ancient village, significantly, on the architectural as on the social unity of the whole.

There is a light but telling stroke which is worth a pause—it will suggest how firmly the novel has been stitched together. Between his discovery of the village in the canyon and his death a few years later Tom made physics his principal study; he devised and patented a bulkheaded vacuum which after his death became the nucleus of a great improvement in aircraft. He had willed everything to his fiancée, one of the professor's daughters, but with not a particle of the professor in her make-up. With some of the immense fortune the invention brought her, she and her husband, a born front-office man, built a country house and called it "Outland." Now the professor's new house is a wrong house, but wrong only by its acceptance of prevailing convention. The memorial to Tom Outland is much more deeply a wrong house. Although it stands on a high site it holds no reminiscence of the village in the canyon —it is a Norwegian manor set down in the sultry Middle West, without a vestige of American feeling. We are spared a sight of its interior; but we are told of what is to furnish it—the loot of the antique shops of Europe imported by way of a Spanish American port in a scheme to evade customs duties.

This is the worst of all the houses in the novel, but there are many modern houses, none of them with any affinity with the village of the Cliff Dwellers. With the kind of past it represents the busy ugly insensitive present seems to have no conceivable bond.

But in the third and final part the bond is suddenly revealed. The first and second parts of the book which have seemed so boldly unrelated are brought into a profound unity. It is in this third part of the novel that the large background of emotion, which demands rhythmic expression if we are to respond to it as it deserves, becomes predominant. In the first part it was plain that the professor did not wish to live in his new house, and did not wish to enter into the sere phase of his life correlative with it. At the beginning of the third part it becomes plain that he cannot indefinitely continue to make the old attic study the theatre of his life, that he cannot go on prolonging or attempting to prolong his prime, the phase of his life correlative with that. The personality of his mature years—the personality that had expressed itself powerfully and in the main happily in his teaching, his scholarship, his love for his wife, his domesticity—is now quickly receding, and nothing new is flowing in. What begins to dominate St. Peter is something akin to the Cliff Dwellers, something primitive which had ruled him long ago when he was a boy on a pioneer farm in the rough Solomon valley in north-western Kansas. To this primitive being not many things were real; the food, love, and society which make up so much of the splendour in life for Virginia Woolf do not seem to have counted for very much; what counted was nature, and nature seen as a web of life, and finally of death.

The essential passage, the binding passage, is in terms of houses, and I do not know of any interpreter who has made use of it:

The Professor really didn't see what he was going to do about the matter of domicile. He couldn't make himself believe that he was ever going to live in the new house again. He didn't belong there. He remembered some lines of a translation from the Norse he used to read long ago in one of his mother's few books, a little two-volume Ticknor and Fields edition of Longfellow, in blue and gold, that used to lie on the parlour table:

> For thee a house was built
> Ere thou wast born;
> For thee a mould was made
> Ere thou of woman camest.[1]

Lying on his old couch he could almost believe himself in that house already. The sagging springs were like the sham upholstery that is put in coffins. Just the equivocal American way of dealing with serious facts, he reflected. Why pretend that it is possible to soften that last hard bed?

He could remember a time when the loneliness of death had terrified him, when the idea of it was insupportable. He used to feel that if his wife could but lie in the same coffin with him, his body would not be so insensible that the nearness of hers would not give it comfort. But now he thought of eternal solitude with gratefulness; as a release from every obligation, from every form of effort. It was the Truth.

All that had seemed a hanging back from the future—the clinging to the old attic study, the absorption in Tom Outland and in the civilization of the Cliff Dwellers, the revival of interest in the occupations of his childhood and its pleasures—was something very unlike what it had seemed. It was profound, unconscious preparation for death, for the last house of the professor.

Again, I believe, the great chords are sounding. Willa Cather had begun on the surface, with a record of mediocrities, of the airless prosaic world of a small college town—how airless, how prosaic only those who have lived in one can know. The mediocrities do not

[1] Miss Cather was quoting from memory the opening of Longfellow's translation of the Anglo-Saxon "Grave":

> For thee was a house built
> Ere thou wast born,
> For thee was a mould meant
> Ere thou of mother camest.

have everything their own way: against them is Professor St. Peter, and he is not quite alone. He is not confined to the here and the now: he has on him the mark of Mediterranean civilization—he almost looks like a Latin—and the mark of the Spanish explorers. Still, the professor and those who are more or less of his stripe are not dominant in this first book; they appear to belong to a minority weak in force as well as in numbers, and close to extinction. Then in the second book Willa Cather inverted the roles. The mediocrities are few and weak; and against them is the revelation of life as the Cliff Dwellers' village records and suggests it. More boldly, more simply than Virginia Woolf she sings the splendour of life.

The surprise for the reader who really reads the novel is not the startling intercalated story: it is the strange short third part. The common quality between life in the Middle Western college town and life in the Cliff Dwellers' village is that both kinds of life end in death. That is something for which neither the first nor the second part of the novel had prepared us. Dominated by the feeling that both kinds of life end in death, we know how to measure them, the ancient and the contemporary. What aspect of dignity, of beauty, would the ruins of the college town possess for Macaulay's New Zealander if he were to pause on this continent on his way to sketch the ruins of St. Paul's? Great chords are sounding; and as they sound they alter radically the impression we had before we approached the end of the novel. I do not wish to press a musical analogy here, or anywhere else in these discourses; but perhaps it may be said that in *To the Lighthouse* the arrangement of the themes and their interweaving are conventional according to sonata form, but that the arrangement and interweaving in *The Professor's House*, with the shock, the revelation in the final part, are highly and stirringly experimental.

III

The mention of great chords sounding is a reminder of the novel that led E. M. Forster to allude to them, *War and Peace*. In that book, complex and varied without a parallel in prose fiction, can a thematic structure be discerned?

When one looks carefully at the structure of *War and Peace*, I believe that the deepest impression is of a movement, at first very slow, finally almost precipitate, from separateness to union. In the first of the fifteen parts into which Tolstoy divides the novel, he puts before us the secure civilized life of St. Petersburg, Moscow, and the estate of Prince Nicholas Bolkonski at Bald Hills. In the second he shifts to the Russian army centred not far from Prague. The young prince Andrew Bolkonski, attached to the staff of Kutuzov, the commander in chief, and the young count Nicholas Rostov of the Pavlograd Hussars are very conscious how far they are from home. As the story shifts back and forth between the army and the families at home, the world of war and the world of peace seem as separate as the world of the Cliff Dwellers and the world of the college town. But Tolstoy brings his two worlds forcibly and dramatically together. Andrew Bolkonski, retiring on Borodino, is following a highway that comes within a few miles of Bald Hills; he rides up to his home to bid the family leave at once. Then, gravely wounded at

Borodino, he is sheltered in the Rostov house in Moscow, and accompanies the Rostovs in the exodus from that city. Nicholas Rostov also rides up to the house at Bald Hills, from the temporary quarters of his retreating regiment; he helps Mary Bolkonski to depart, and falls in love with her. Andrew Bolkonski has long been in love with Natasha Rostov; but it is now, in the late parts of the novel, with the world of war and the world of peace interweaving more and more intimately, fusing with each other, that his love and hers come to the height.

The movement from separateness to union is also expressed in political and intellectual terms. The first scene in the novel, that unforgettable soirée at St. Petersburg before war is declared, introduces Andrew Bolkonski and his friend Pierre Bezukhov. Both are admirers of Napoleon and his great designs. Their admiration separates them from the general sympathies of their countrymen. The movement of the novel will show them turning from Napoleon and becoming Russian to the marrow. The spirit of Russia is chiefly, or most conspicuously, embodied in two men, the commander in chief Kutuzov, and a simple near-pauper Platon Karataev. Andrew Bolkonski becomes more and more a disciple of Kutuzov; wounded and left for dead at Austerlitz, he is greeted courteously by Napoleon, but not a vestige of Bolkonski's admiration remains—it has given place to contempt. Pierre Bezukhov stays on in Moscow after the exodus, with the intention of assassinating Napoleon; taken prisoner he comes to know Karataev and to prize his wisdom above anything else.

The wisdom of Karataev and the wisdom of Kutuzov are one. At the end of the first section in the first epilogue Tolstoy has this sentence: "If we admit that human life can be ruled by reason, the possibility of life is destroyed." Napoleon is the supreme case of reason in the novel. He is the man of plans and designs, the man who believes that the reason of an individual expressed in plans and designs can shape the course of history. Kutuzov's staff abounds in generals who share this belief; Tolstoy relishes repeating their alien names: Bennigsen, Toll, Barclay de Tolly, Wintzengerode, Pfuel. Pfuel was the purest planner of all on the Russian side, "the German theorist in whom all the characteristics of those others were united. He had a science—the theory of oblique movements deduced by him from the history of Frederick the Great's wars, and all he came across in the history of more recent warfare seemed to him absurd and barbarous—monstrous collisions in which so many blunders were committed by both sides that these wars could not be called wars, they did not accord with the theory, and therefore could not serve as material for science." Such a theoretical madness was the antithesis of the truly Russian approach. Pfuel fancied that he possessed the truth, the absolute truth, and what he possessed was merely the theory he had invented. A Russian, on the other hand, "knows nothing and does not want to know anything, since he does not believe that anything can be known." Kutuzov was such a person. When a general expounded a complicated strategy he listened as little as he could, on one occasion he had stuffed an ear with tow; when documents were left with him he groaned, and when alone again either dozed or read a French novel. In describing what Kutuzov depended on, instead of on reason, Tolstoy is in the difficulty that dogs all anti-rationalists:

the various anti-rational beliefs are all damaged when
put into words. Kutuzov depended on intuition, and
his intuition took account of his vast experience of men
and war, but most of all, of his mysterious sense of
Russian character and temperament. He was, and he
was felt to be, the embodiment of the people. Kutuzov
always knew what his armies and his generals could do,
and what it was futile to ask of them. He was profoundly in relation to everyone—he had not the shell
of personal ideas and intentions that separates a man
from others. He did not try to prevent Pfuel from
elaborating plans—to elaborate plans was the nature
of the beast. He was content with delaying their execu-
tion until they were inapplicable. Karataev too was
without a shell of personal ideas and intentions. He
was, says Tolstoy, "the personification of everything
Russian, kindly, and round," "an unfathomable,
rounded, eternal personification of the spirit of sim-
plicity and truth." Like Kutuzov he speaks and acts as
his heart at the moment bids him act, impulsive, unconscious of motive or aim, simply expressing the content of his being. This content, as Tolstoy believes, is
what the facts of the immediate situation present to a
man who has stripped himself of the layers of personal
ideas and intentions that ordinarily distort one's sense
of the outer world. Men like Kutuzov and Karataev are
models just because they are not separated persons, but
organs for the expression of the nature of things. I am
sorry to fall into the language of romantic mysticism, or
"the vertigo of oriental asceticism" as the Vicomte de
Vogüé calls it, but it is less romantically mystical than
Tolstoy's who says of Karataev: "Every word and action
of his was the manifestation of an activity unknown to

him, which was his life. But his life, as he regarded it, had no meaning as a separate thing. It had meaning only as part of a whole of which he was always conscious. His words and actions flowed from him as evenly, inevitably, and spontaneously as fragrance exhales from a flower. He could not understand the value or significance of any word or deed taken separately." These two profoundly Russian men Kutuzov and Karataev, men who have lost their separateness and become united with the nature of things, help Andrew Bolkonski and Pierre Bezukhov, in whom separate personalities had been developed to an unusual degree by their nervous energy, their tense aims, their preoccupation with ideas, to come out of their shells, to abandon reason and appreciate fact, to pass from what destroys to what calms and enriches.

The movement from separateness to union is also expressed in the rise of the Rostov family. Of all the families in the novel only the Rostovs have the qualities that make for union and enable others to escape from separateness. This is their charm as it was Mrs. Ramsay's and it is felt by everyone who matters. Although they are not exempt from misfortune—nor were Kutuzov and Karataev—they are the winners at the end of the chronicle. Andrew Bolkonski would have married Natasha Rostov if he had lived; Pierre marries her. Andrew's sister marries Nicholas Rostov. In the first epilogue Tolstoy shows us the two young families together; and their tone is a Rostov tone, not a tone of intellect, or of spirituality, or of great intentions, but a tone of spontaneous, intense, and kindly life. That life is the life not of separate individuals, but of a group. Mary Bolkonski retains her spirituality and Pierre retains his zeal for social reform; people cannot be wholly remade; but neither Mary nor Pierre suffers from separateness as both had done until they met examples of union.

The movement from separateness to union flows through many other corners of the novel, through every corner, but I may not now go into all its effects. What I required to do was to show that in *War and Peace* as in *To the Lighthouse* and *The Professor's House*, there is an interplay through the phases of the novel of two great forces, and a resolution in favour of one. In the interplay everything has its role: not only the catalogue of strategies that is E. M. Forster's instance of a seeming excrescence—it would not be mine, but all Pierre Bezukhov's concern with the Masonic lodges, institutions aiming at union but failing because most of the individuals within them cling to their separating designs and hopes; and even the hunting scenes on the Rostov estate, at the end of which the kindly warmth and impulsiveness of the young Rostovs are so heightened that Nicholas and Natasha can identify themselves happily and uncritically with an old cousin who is ending his days in a rough provincial way that is superficially immoral. Nothing is really excrescent in this amazing book; everything is woven in; and when I reread it my sense of its unity through all the variations of its themes is what most of all persuades me that not a page may be skimmed without loss to one's total impression.

Tolstoy's use of themes is very unlike Virginia Woolf's and Willa Cather's. Like many other anti-rationalists he is a devotee of argument; he is seldom content to allow his opposition of separateness and union to work on a reader's feelings solely through the evolution of the themes. He intends also to prove the error of separateness, as in his demonstration that Napoleon lost the Russian campaign because his trust and pride in reason robbed him of a sense for fact, and in the accompanying demonstration that Kutuzov's strategy of delay and evasion was the ideal plan for the complex circumstances in which Kutuzov was involved and which he felt with unerring truth. Tolstoy's skill and pleasure in argument reduce the part played by the interweaving of his themes, and for some readers who are better at apprehending ideas than at responding to emotions, the themes are obscured. When Forster, who is not, need I say? a reader of this kind, objects to the catalogue of strategies it is, I think, because he feels that Tolstoy is giving argument where he might better be rendering emotion through the themes.

The role of the themes is also affected, and profoundly, by Tolstoy's pleasure in a structure much less regular than Virginia Woolf's or Willa Cather's. His structure is indeed so irregular, so flexible, that readers who prefer, with Percy Lubbock, to feel the guiding pressure of structure in a novel, do not find in *War and Peace* a structural whole. It is a whole, only that whole extends over so vast an area that its limits are sometimes invisible and some of its configurations blurred. The demand upon the reader's aesthetic perceptions is greater than Virginia Woolf or Willa Cather required to make: is not the pleasure for the reader whose perceptions are adequate to the demand the richer?[1]

[1] In passing I must notice a remark that Forster makes in another chapter of the *Aspects of the Novel*. He finds the power of *War and Peace* depending not so much on people or episodes or plot as on the use of space, "the immense area of Russia, over which episodes

IV

The interweaving of themes is the most complex among the kinds of repetition with variation in the novel. Like the expanding symbol it solicits the reader's attention for something beyond the particular set of people, the particular sequence of events, the particular concatenation of settings. In *To the Lighthouse* we are guided beyond the life and death of Mrs. Ramsay to the forces making for life and death throughout organic nature. In *The Professor's House* we are guided beyond the college town and the Cliff Dwellers' village, beyond the professor and Tom Outland and their researches, to the fate they have in common with all mankind. In *War and Peace* neither the fate of individuals or families, nor the outcome of the most terrible conflict known to Tolstoy can finally arrest our attention: that moves on to contemplate the nature of conflict and of family and individual fate. The interweaving of themes is one of the most powerful, one of the most convincing and moving means for generalizing a novelist's effect. Some novelists generalize the effect with a much

and characters have been scattered, the sum-total of bridges and frozen rivers, forests, roads, gardens, fields, which accumulate grandeur and sonority after we have passed them." Forster's language here, the reference to an accumulation of grandeur and sonority that moves us after we have passed the detail and can fit it into a general effect, links his emphasis on the use of space with his notion of the rhythmic, with thematic structure.

It is in space, not in time, that Tolstoy places his two great opposing forces. Space separates; it is not as tragic a cause of separation as time; but only when space has been overcome can there be union. The novel abounds in incidents that show how disastrous is separation by space, and how one person's attitude towards another is improved when they come into each other's presence. A slight, but most moving example is what happens when Pierre Bezukhov is brought before Marshal Davout.

blunter instrument, explicit comment. That is the usual Victorian means. At the end of *Middlemarch* George Eliot wrote of "insignificant people with our daily words and acts preparing the lives of many Dorotheas, some of which may present a far sadder sacrifice than that of the Dorothea whose story we know," and in the final words, "that things are not so ill with you and me as they might have been, is half owing to the number who lived faithfully a hidden life, and rest in unvisited tombs." In this vein, generalizing the matter of the novel, or a part of it, and thus bringing its significance sharply home to the reader, there are scores of passages in Dickens and Thackeray, and indeed in their French contemporaries. Or the effect may be generalized by the choice of a title, by adopting *A Hero of Our Times* instead of *Pechórin,* or *The Way of All Flesh* instead of *Ernest Pontifex.* There is no end to the listing of means for generalizing an effect.

But what none of these blunt means that have been mentioned achieves, and what the kinds of repetition with or without variation considered in the first discourse do not achieve, is the implication of mystery. The link between expanding symbols and interweaving themes is in the implication that beyond what the novelist has been able to set forth there is another area, only glimpsed, not surveyed, a mystery but not a muddle. "Mystery" and "muddle" are favourite terms of E. M. Forster's; and in setting them against each other I had in mind a remark of Mrs. Moore's in *A Passage to India*: "I like mysteries, but I rather dislike muddles." The last of these discourses will touch on the several forms of the rhythmic process in that extraordinary novel.

IV

RHYTHM IN E. M. FORSTER'S
A PASSAGE TO INDIA

NOVELIST may use many kinds of rhythm in one work. In this last discourse I propose to consider one work, to touch on the varied forms of the device, and to inquire briefly into the effect that comes from the combination of phrases, characters, and incidents, rhythmically arranged, with a profusion of expanding symbols, and with a complex evolution of themes.

The one work is E. M. Forster's *A Passage to India,* and I may as well say now that I believe it to be a great novel. It is so unlike most great novels that for a long time I thought of it as remarkable rather than great. After many rereadings, always finding more in the work than I had before, I have changed my mind. One of the reasons why I set *A Passage to India* so high will, perhaps; appear in these pages: its greatness is intimately dependent on E. M. Forster's mastery of expanding symbols and thematic structure, and on that element in his spirit for which expanding symbols and thematic structure are appropriate language.

One of the first examples I gave of repetition with variation was from *Esther Waters*: the word-for-word repetition late in the book of the first paragraph, followed by the repetition with significant variation of the second paragraph. In *A Passage to India* there is something very like this, but subtle as well as emphatic.

In the second chapter of Forster's novel characters

begin to appear. There is Aziz, the Mohammedan physician, engaged in friendly argument with Mohammedan
friends: "they were discussing as to whether or no
it is possible to be friends with an Englishman." The
conclusion is that in India, at least, friendship with the
invader is impossible, unpermitted. Aziz is summoned
to his chief, the Civil Surgeon, Dr. Callendar, and on
the steps of Callendar's bungalow suffers a slight from
two Anglo-Indian women. As they come out on the
verandah he lifts his hat; instinctively they turn away.
They jump into the carriage he has hired and are about
to drive off without asking consent. Aziz says "You
are most welcome, ladies"; they do not think of reply-
ing. The Civil Surgeon has left, and there is no message.
Aziz takes his injured feelings to the mosque, and in
the night's coolness he meditates upon the past of Islam.
He recalls a Persian inscription he had once seen on the
tomb of a Deccan king, especially these closing lines:

> But those who have secretly understood my heart—
> They will approach and visit the grave where I lie.

As he is repeating the words "the secret understanding
of the heart" in the one place in Chandrapore where he
was sure no European would intrude, an Englishwoman
steps into the moonlight. Aziz rages at her. But Mrs.
Moore has done the right thing, has removed her shoes
—says the right thing, "God is here"—and in a minute
they are friends. They talk of their children, of people
round about, of India, of religion. "The flame that not
even beauty can nourish" was springing up in Aziz, for
this red-faced old woman; and when she remarks "I
don't think I understand people very well. I only know
whether I like or dislike them," Aziz declares: "Then
you are an Oriental." He has learned that one can be

friends with an Englishman, even with an Englishwoman, and in India. Two years later when the novel
is about to close, Aziz repeats the declaration. Not to
Mrs. Moore—she is dead—but to her son, the young
boy Ralph.

Aziz is no longer in British India. He has resolved to
have no more to do with the invader, and is physician
to the rajah of a Hindu state. Into a seclusion even
deeper than that of the mosque where he had met Mrs.
Moore, once more the English penetrate. One of the
intruders is Ralph, who is stung by bees. So great is
Aziz' hatred of the English that he is sadistically happy
to have an English boy in his power. He will treat him
with the savagery the Civil Surgeon had used towards
the young son of a Nawab. Ralph astonishes Aziz with
a most unEnglish expression: "Your hands are unkind."
The memory of Mrs. Moore floods in, expelling all
hatred. Aziz bids Ralph a gentle good-bye, and Ralph
responds with equal gentleness. Aziz asks "Can you
always tell whether a stranger is your friend?" "Yes,"
Ralph replies simply. "Then you are an Oriental"—the
words are drawn out of Aziz, and he is appalled. "He
unclasped as he spoke, with a little shudder. Those
words—he had said them to Mrs. Moore in the mosque
in the beginning of the cycle, from which, after so much
suffering, he had got free." Instead of the good-bye Aziz
had planned, and the hurried escape from reinvolve-
ment with the English, he talks with Ralph about Mrs.
Moore and in friendship takes the boy out on the
water, as in friendship he had taken Mrs. Moore to the
Marabar Caves. What they say of Mrs. Moore, and
what befalls them on the water I am not yet ready to
consider. But the cycle is clearly beginning again. The

effect that George Moore sought in *Esther Waters,* and achieved, was of a closing in of the life in his tale; the effect in *A Passage to India* is of an opening out of life. It is as if at the point where one circle was completed, another and larger circle immediately began.

Ralph Moore serves in another kind of rhythmic process. I used the two daughters in *Le Père Goriot* and the two in *A Lear of the Steppes* as examples of a pair of characters radically alike in nature and in function. Balzac's daughters have only surface differences; with Turgenev's there is also gradation, a significant difference in the degree to which they are mastered by the same ruling passion, and a surprise. The likeness between Ralph Moore and his mother, profound, intimate, mysterious, is a gradation and a surprise of Turgenev's sort. Ralph is a prolongation of his mother. He is a simpler person because he lacks the shell of practical sense and adaptability which hid her essential nature from almost everyone until "India brought her into the open." It may be said of Ralph that he is what his mother is so far as she eternally matters. The repetition of Mrs. Moore in the two children of her second marriage—for Ralph's sister Stella is of the same substance, although she remains a faint figure—hits the reader more strongly since the child of the first marriage, the only one of her children to appear in the early and middle parts of the book, derives nothing from his mother. Ronnie Heaslop, bureaucrat, conventionalist, empire-builder, snob, is a thorough Wilcox. He could have changed places with the younger Wilcox boy and no one would have noticed the shift. Especially to one who reads *A Passage to India* after reading *Howards End* the prolongation of Mrs. Moore in her youngest child is emotionally effective. It is a vehicle for the mystery in which the meaning of *A Passage to India* is so deeply engaged.

II

I mentioned the bee-stings which led to Ralph's encounter with Aziz. They will take us to one of the expanding symbols.

Early in the novel, on the evening when she had met Aziz at the mosque, Mrs. Moore is undressing in her son's bungalow. As she is about to hang up her cloak she notices that on the tip of the peg is a wasp, a quite unEnglish wasp, an "Indian Social Wasp."

Perhaps he mistook the peg for a branch—no Indian animal has any sense of an interior. Bats, rats, birds, insects will as soon nest inside a house as out; it is to them a normal growth of the eternal jungle, which alternately produces houses trees, houses trees. There he clung, asleep, while jackals in the plain bayed their desires and mingled with the percussion of drums.

"Pretty dear," said Mrs. Moore to the wasp. He did not wake, but her voice floated out, to swell the night's uneasiness.

There the chapter ends. If you read these lines in the context they take on certain precise meanings. Mrs. Moore had divided her evening between the English club (where no native was allowed) and the mosque (where no English folk came). None of the sundried Anglo-Indians would have called the wasp a pretty dear; all of them would have been irritated by the wasp's inability to discriminate a house from a tree, which is India's inability, India's disinclination, to make the sharp tidy distinctions by which the Western intelligence operates. At the club that evening the talk had turned to religion. The Civil Surgeon's wife had said

that the kindest thing one could do for a native was to
let him die. Mrs. Moore had inquired, with a "crooked
smile," what if he went to heaven? A woman who had
been a nurse in a native state was ready for this with
a razor-sharp distinction: "I am all for Chaplains, but
all against Missionaries." The little incident with which
the evening closes epitomizes Mrs. Moore's behaviour
at the club and at the mosque, her indifference to sharp
distinctions, her instinctive affection and consideration.
But this, and other precise meanings in her approach
to the wasp do not exhaust the force or account for the
charm of the passage. The disturbing noises which accompany Mrs. Moore's gesture of affection and consideration—the minatory baying of the jackals and percussion of the drums offer an undertone of suggestion
that, unexpectedly beautiful and adequate as Mrs.
Moore's response to Aziz and to the wasp had been,
there are ordeals ahead to which even Mrs. Moore may
be insufficient.

Late in the novel, long after her death, the wasp returns, or rather it is now the idea of the wasp. The
Brahman Godbole, at the climactic moment in the book,
is attempting union with the divine. He does so in a
ceremony that could satisfy no Western person. It is a
ceremony abounding in jumble, amorphousness. Each
of the noisy corybantic worshippers is inviting the return of the strongest, purest attachments in his experience. "Thus Godbole, though she was not important
to him, remembered an old woman he had met in
Chandrapore days. . . . she happened to occur among
the throng of soliciting images, a tiny splinter, and he
impelled her by his spiritual force to that place where
completeness can be found." Having impelled Mrs.

Moore triumphantly to her place, he tried again. "His senses grew thinner, he remembered a wasp seen he forgot where, perhaps on a stone. He loved the wasp equally, he impelled it likewise, he was imitating God." There his triumph flared out. He found he could do nothing with the stone, arbitrarily, superficially, cognitively associated with the wasp. "'One old Englishwoman and one little, little wasp,' he thought, as he stepped out of the temple into the grey of a pouring wet morning. 'It does not seem much, still it is more than I am myself.'"

Just what is achieved by the recurrence of the wasp? To have shown Godbole triumphantly impelling Mrs. Moore would have established the effect that is most obviously needed: that of an affinity between Godbole and the old Englishwoman who has not come so far as he along the mystical path. In the novel they have but one important interchange—an interchange of spiritual ideas—and apart from this they scarcely see each other. They do not wish to, do not need to. Godbole's recollection of her at a spiritual moment crucial for him establishes that one interchange is enough. It tells us something that for E. M. Forster is most important about human relationships. All this, and more perhaps, can be achieved without the recurrence of the wasp.

The recurrence of the wasp does not point, as one of my students once suggested, to Professor Godbole's having taken an unrecorded walk by Mrs. Moore's window when she was undressing. The recurrence of the wasp points to an identity in the objects to which the analogous characters were drawn. That each should have been powerfully attracted to something so apparently trivial as a wasp suggests that they were not

only alike but mysteriously alike. Because of the wasp
we appear to be in the presence of something so elusive
that we cannot understand it, that we brood about it
with a conviction that it contains some kernel of meaning we do not know how to extract. It can be said of
the wasp as E. M. Forster said of Vinteuil's music that
it has a life of its own, that it is almost an actor in the
novel but not quite.

Between its two big moments the wasp is not wholly
neglected. Not all the English in Forster's India adopt
the prejudices of the official classes. The nurse from the
native state was opposed to missionaries; but the missionaries in Chandrapore are more sensitive, more
human, than the mass of their countrymen. In a review
printed four years before the novel Forster wrote: "It is
the missionary rather than the Government official who
is in touch with native opinion. The official need only
learn how people can be governed. The missionary,
since he wants to alter them, must learn what they are."
The missionaries never came to the club at Chandrapore, and on principle they used the third-class cars on
the trains. The call to salvation, they knew and taught
and lived, was addressed to all mankind. But what,
their Indian friends would ask, of the animals? Were
there mansions in heaven for the monkeys? The elder
missionary thought not, but the younger was liberal,
and "saw no reason why monkeys should not have their
collateral share of bliss." As the conversation descended
below the mammalian the younger missionary felt less
at ease, and when the wasp was mentioned he was
prone to change the subject. The call of the Western
intelligence for a razor-sharp distinction became im-
perious. "We must exclude someone from our gathering,

or we shall be left with nothing." The use of the wasp in this passage beautifully underlines by contrast the spiritual agreement between the Brahman and the contemplative Christian Mrs. Moore: for them the divine call has no fixed exclusions—would not be divine if it had.

And then there are the bees with which I began. They live in the shrine of a Mohammedan saint, who had freed prisoners, and when the police intervened and cut off his head, "ignored" this misadventure and slew as many of them as were about. The shrine is not a mosque, but there is a miniature mosque beside it. We are brought back to the encounter between Aziz and Mrs. Moore at the beginning of the novel. The sudden rage of the bees against the intruders is like Aziz' sudden rage against her; and it ends as quickly. The rage of the bees seems to suggest that subhuman India is hostile to interracial friendships, a suggestion repeated with virtuosity throughout the book, and nowhere so forcibly as in the final paragraph. Aziz and the Englishman he has liked most, Cyril Fielding, are riding in the country. Aziz, in a sudden spurt of affection, pulls his horse so close to Fielding's that he can half kiss him; and Fielding responds by holding Aziz affectionately.

But the horses didn't want it—they swerved apart; the earth didn't want it, sending up rocks through which riders must pass single file; the temples, the tank, the jail, the palace, the birds, the carrion, the Guest House, that came into view as they issued from the gap and saw Mau beneath: they didn't want it, they said in their hundred voices, "No, not yet," and the sky said, "No, not there."

Clearly, the bees are divisive as the wasps are not. And yet the bees are not merely divisive—they were the occasion for the personal relation between Aziz and

Ralph Moore, just as the wasp was, not indeed the occasion, but the evidence of mystery in the personal relation between Godbole and Mrs. Moore.

The greatest of the expanding symbols in *A Passage to India* is the echo. The most lasting among the effects of the visit that Mrs. Moore and Adela Quested made to the Marabar Caves as the guests of Aziz was the echo. Mrs. Moore disliked the echo when she was in the one cave she entered; but after she had emerged and had had time to arrange her impressions she minded it much more. "The echo began in some indescribable way to undermine her hold on life." It blurred all distinctions, and even Mrs. Moore had enough of the West in her to become uneasy. To the highest poetry and the coarsest obscenity the echo would have offered the same reply—"ou-boum." Other Indian echoes, Forster pauses to insist, are quite different; at Mandu long sentences will journey through the air and return to their speaker intact. At the Marabar the utterance is reduced to the dullness of one flat response mercilessly reiterated. Mrs. Moore found that the echo voided of all meaning the past, present, and future of her life. The echo disturbed Adela Quested's steady balance. Love and marriage were on her mind as she moved towards the second cave, and she suffered the delusion that Aziz, who did not in fact care for her in any way except as an honoured guest, attempted to rape her.

The reader has been lured into pondering about echoes before they dominate the crucial scene at the caves. The Collector, the principal English official at Chandrapore, learning that Mrs. Moore and Miss Quested wish to meet "the Aryan Brother," gives what he calls a "Bridge Party" for the leading local people

of both colours. In vain do the two visitors from England
try to bridge a gap, crossing from the side of the garden
chosen by the pinko-greys, as Fielding calls them, to
the side where India seems to promise revelations to
anyone bold enough to seek. Mrs. Moore and Miss
Quested make special efforts with two Hindu women;
but everything dies against "the echoing walls of their
civility." At home the evening after the ineffectual
party Mrs. Moore takes stock of what India has done
for her in a few weeks. It has made her speak more often
of God; but it has also moved the old spiritual land-
marks, and God has seemed a less satisfactory formulation for the content of her belief. "Outside the arch
[and the arch is also a powerful expanding symbol with
which I have not space to deal] there seemed always an
arch, beyond the remotest echo a silence."

As the narrative begins to move directly towards the
Marabar Caves, sounds exercise a decisive effect on the
two women who are to find the echoes in those caves
so disturbing. The Brahman Godbole concludes a tea
party at Fielding's by singing a song whose spiritual
content is as bemusing as its form is at variance with
Western conceptions of music. The Englishwomen are
so affected by his song that in the days intervening
between their hearing it and their starting for the caves
they exist as if in cocoons. On the local train that takes
them to the Marabar the dull repetitive sound of the
wheels has an effect prefiguring the echo's on Mrs.
Moore. "Pomper, pomper, pomper," say the wheels and
rob Adela Quested's sentences and ideas of any distinct-
ness. On another line not far away the crack mail train
that linked Calcutta with Lahore shot along with a
shriek that meant business. That shriek Adela could have

understood, it was of her world; but with "pomper, pomper, pomper" she can do nothing. Unless one can do something, even do a great deal, with "pomper, pomper, pomper," one can do nothing with India. For the meanings of India are indistinct and repetitive. Until the Western visitor can make something of the indistinctness indefinitely repeated, he can neither comprehend any of the meanings of India nor begin to cope with them. India, says Forster, is not a promise, it is nothing so definite, it is only an appeal.

The indistinctness and repetitiveness, exasperating to a Western mind, are beautifully captured at the beginning of a notice that in 1919 Forster wrote for the *Athenaeum*. The book reviewed was *Hindu and Buddhist Monuments, Northern Circle,* published by the Mysore Archaeological Department.

> "Ought we not to start? The elephants must be waiting."
> "There is no necessity. Elephants sometimes wait four hours."
> "But the Temple is far."
> "Oh no, there are thirty of them."
> "Thirty temples! Are they far?"
> "No, no, no, not at all—fifteen really, but much jungle; fifteen to come and fifteen to go."
> "Fifteen of what?"
> "Fifteen all."

> After such preparations, and in such a spirit, the Temple used to be attacked; and came off victorious. Whether it was one, or fifteen or thirty, or thirty miles off, was never proved, because the elephant misunderstood, or plans changed, or tiffin was too delicious. Evening fell, and the pale blue dome of the sky was corniced with purple where it touched the trees. "It will now be too late for the Temple." So it keeps its secret in some stony gorge or field of tough grass, or, more triumphant still, in the land beyond either, where a mile and an elephant are identical and everything is nothing.

The Mysore Archaeological Department does not approach a monument in this instinctive fashion. It is as precise, as Western, as Aziz' plans for the expedition to the Marabar Caves. Aziz worked out a schedule that would honour the secretary of a national convention: transport, food, seating, even jokes, were minutely arranged. Lest he and his servants be late they spend the preceding night at the station. India is too much for them. Fielding and Godbole miss the train; and Mrs. Moore and Miss Quested hate the caves—Mrs. Moore will enter only one of them, Adela only two.

In the caves the indistinct meanings of India have agglomerated in a form of shocking intensity and explode at the visitors in the horrifying echo. Until she entered a cave Adela Quested had made nothing of these meanings. The most that can be said for her is that unlike the Anglo-Indians she has been aware of bafflement, conscious of a profound uneasiness. Mrs. Moore was not quite so pitifully unprepared: she was spiritually active, moving blindly towards a more adequate formulation of the divine. She too was shattered by the echoes.

For the length of many chapters after the scene at the caves, the echo leaves a disturbing residue in the minds of both Englishwomen. What the residue was I shall inquire when looking at the thematic structure of the novel.

After Mrs. Moore's death and Adela's return to England, the echo begins to matter to Cyril Fielding. When, after the catastrophe, he entered a Marabar cave, the echo had no impact on him. In the hubbub of distorted rumour and opinion released in Chandrapore by Adela's charge against Aziz, Fielding kept his head, and was the only Englishman to do so. It was now his turn to exist within a cocoon—he was enclosed by his intuitive assurance that Aziz could not have done what he was charged with doing. No distorting, dispiriting echo could penetrate that cocoon. When Adela withdrew her charge the Anglo-Indian world at Chandrapore collapsed. But when a new crop of officials arrived they were, Fielding found, just like those who had been withdrawn. After he has met them at the club, Fielding muses: "Everything echoes now; there's no stopping the echo. The original sound may be harmless, but the echo is always evil." On this musing Forster comments: "This reflection about an echo lay at the verge of Fielding's mind. He could never develop it. It belonged to the universe that he had missed or rejected." Indistinct meanings were almost as alien to his fluid but yet Western mind as to the more rigid mind of Adela Quested. What he has, and she has not, is some grasp of the nature of personal relationships. He has shown again and again his appreciation of how attractive personalities falsify themselves and show at their worst when they suffer the impact of aggressive personalities that are antagonistic to them. At the close of his tea party he saw Aziz behaving in a repulsive way—"impertinent" to Ronnie Heaslop, "loud and jolly" to Godbole, "greasily confidential" to Adela Quested—and instead of revising his opinion of Aziz, he merely concluded that something had happened to upset the nervous Mohammedan. Ronnie Heaslop had happened. And what is true of individuals, Fielding's political shrewdness tells him, is more painfully true of national groups and social classes. "The original sound may be harmless, but the echo is always evil."

As the novel approaches a close, Forster introduces perhaps the most moving of all his uses of the echo. In the courtroom scene at the middle of the *Passage,* when

Mrs. Moore's name is mentioned in testimony, the native crowd outside distorts it into "Esmiss Esmoor," and chants these mysterious syllables as if they were the name of a goddess, or the means to salvation. Indeed they are. For it was after the crowd had chanted the distortion that Adela was freed from her delusion, and changing her story, saved Aziz. When at the end Mrs. Moore's younger children fall in with Aziz, the Hindus at their worship are repeating: "Radhakrishna Radhakrishna Krishnaradha Radhakrishna"; and suddenly in the interstices of the chant Aziz "heard, almost certainly, the syllables of salvation that had sounded during his trial at Chandrapore."

The echo, like the bee-wasp symbol, is manifold in meaning. An echo distorts Mrs. Moore's sense of the purport of life, but that distortion, we may shortly see, is not entirely ruinous. An echo distorts Adela's sense of what happened in the cave; but another echo restores her to the truth. Good and evil interweave in these expanding symbols, making them more mysterious; just as we shall see them interweave in the development of the themes.

III

A Passage to India is in three parts. Their titles—"Mosque," "Caves," "Temple"—warn of a meaning which goes behind story, people, even setting. Each part has a curious and beautiful prefatory chapter, and each of these chapters abounds in symbols, abstractions, suggestions. Their full weight of meaning is slow in revealing itself; indeed I am not sure that any reader of the novel will ever possess all that has been flung into these chapters.

It is obvious that they are in balance. They also inter-weave. The first chapter in the part called "Mosque" begins: "Except for the Marabar Caves" and ends "These fists and fingers are the Marabar Hills, contain-ing the extraordinary caves." There is a reference to temples tucked away in a detailed catalogue of the topography of Chandrapore. To mosques the only refer-ence is in the title for this part of the novel, standing at the top of the opening page and then used as a running head. The first chapter of the part called "Caves" has no backward glance towards the mosque or any element of the Moslem faith; but it is packed with suggestive remarks that point forward to the temple and the Hindu faith; and these are sharply in contrast with the chief substance of the chapter, the account of an India far older than Moslem or Hindu, whose faith has left a mysterious residue in the primitive Marabar Caves. The first chapter of the part called "Temple" opens as the first chapter of "Mosque" opened, with a reference to the caves; and the Moslem element is gathered in by the importance to the action in the chapter of the chief Moslem person in the novel, Aziz. In the inter-weaving of elements in these prefatory chapters there is increasing complication but no petty mechanical bal-ancing, no sterile exactness of repetition. Vitality is not sacrificed to pattern.

It is useful to look at the prefatory chapters as a group; seen in this way they offer an initiation into the kind of approach the three parts of the novel will best respond to. What has appeared in the chapters will be recognized, although not so readily, in the three big blocks that compose *A Passage to India*.

In the first of these blocks we are brought to a

mosque; in the second to the caves; in the third to a temple. Each visit has consequences which linger through the rest of the novel. The novel thus becomes progressively more complex. In the first block not only is the Moslem element dominant—it far outweighs the caves and the temple; all that we get about caves and temple is preparatory. At the other extreme, in the third block, where the Hindu element is dominant, the persistence of the Moslem and of that more primitive and elusive element represented by the caves is multiform and of a kind to command a great part of the reader's attention and emotion.

In her visit to the mosque at Chandrapore Mrs. Moore enters with a happy and intuitive adequacy into an understanding of the Moslem element. She leaves the stifling club late in the evening and approaches the mosque alone. We have seen how easily she enters into a personal understanding of Aziz. The understanding so quickly and strangely established endures throughout the novel. She never doubts that Aziz is innocent of the charge Adela brings against him. In the next to last chapter Aziz tells Ralph Moore: "Yes, your mother was my best friend in all the world." "He was silent," the passage continues, "puzzled by his own great gratitude. What did this eternal goodness of Mrs. Moore amount to? To nothing, if brought to the test of thought. She had not borne witness in his favour [Adela had done that], nor visited him in the prison [Fielding had done that], yet she had stolen to the depths of his heart, and he always adored her." To return to the images in Helen Schlegel's interpretation of the Fifth Symphony, the goblins have no power whatever over the relation between Mrs. Moore and Aziz. When he first saw her white form in the darkness of the mosque, he had been repeating to himself in Persian "the secret understanding of the heart." So far as the main meaning of the first block in the novel admits of formulation, there is the formula.

Before the second part of the novel has begun, at Fielding's tea party (an indirect outcome of the meeting at the mosque) the Marabar Caves begin to threaten. Aziz has never seen them, nor has he any knowledge of them beyond common report. But when the English visitors express a wish to see more of India, and see more deeply, he proposes an expedition to the caves. He asks the Brahman Godbole to describe them. Godbole confines himself to brief negatives. The caves contain no sculpture, no ornament of any kind; nor are they especially holy. To every effort Aziz makes to discover why the caves are worth seeing, Godbole is impenetrable. The comparatively simple mind of the Mohammedan, we are told, "was encountering Ancient Night." It is an ominous and mysterious overture. Godbole is invited to join the expedition, and agrees; but when the time comes he prolongs his prayers, innocently misses the train, and makes Fielding miss it too. The visitors from England approach the caves under the guidance of Aziz, the blind led by the blind.

The caves are in an outpost of the high places of Dravidia, which were land when the oceans covered the holy places of Hindustan, before there was a Ganges, before there were Himalayas. Forster has moved them some hundreds of miles, as he tells us in a note to the "Everyman" edition, doubtless to bring them within reach of the Ganges where for many reasons he prefers to situate the early and middle parts of his story. The hills in which they lie were flesh of the sun's flesh, their contours never softened by the flow of water, and some of the edges and masses they had when they belonged to the sun they still preserve. The hills, like so many of the aspects of India, strike Forster as violating the beauties of proportion and thus certain to confuse and depress a European. When Cyril Fielding returns to Europe at the end of the second block of the novel he lands at Venice after a stay in Egypt and a sight of Crete. "The buildings of Venice," he noted, "like the mountains of Crete and the fields of Egypt, stood in the right place, whereas in poor India everything was placed wrong. He had forgotten the beauty of form among idol temples and lumpy hills." The Marabar Hills are lumpy; they rise "abruptly, insanely, without the proportion that is kept by the wildest hills elsewhere." Mrs. Moore and Miss Quested did not find them attractive or interesting; they could not see why these hills should have a reputation and draw people to look on them. They did not understand that to lack form is not simply a negation: that the vacuum left is filled by something else, elusive but perhaps of equal importance.

What Forster is doing in the description of the hills, and later of the caves, is easy to formulate if one is content with general terms. He is taking his characters beyond their depth; the minds of Mrs. Moore and Miss Quested, Western, modern, complex, cannot operate on the level of primitivism which the hills and the caves exemplify. Mrs. Moore is not so much at a loss as Miss Quested, even momentarily, for she is less Western, less modern, even less complex. Miss Quested's mind goes wild and she makes the absurd charge against Aziz;

Mrs. Moore's mind goes dead—she is aware of its incompetence, aware that in the circumstances of the caves and hills it cannot operate at all. The secret understanding of the heart is no longer enough.

The echo in a Marabar cave is almost exactly like the utterance of the goblins in the Fifth Symphony, a denial of human values, in this case by way of a denial of all distinctions. "Pathos, piety, courage—they exist, but are identical, and so is filth," the echo persuades Mrs. Moore. "Everything exists, nothing has value." Panic and emptiness were what the goblins infused into Helen Schlegel listening to Beethoven in the Queen's Hall; and the echo infuses them into Mrs. Moore. Emptiness. The relations that have made hers a full life—her affection for her children, her devotion to God—have suddenly snapped. She could not—and this happens in a moment—interest herself in the fortunes of her children, either in those of the son at Chandrapore or in those of the younger two in England. The Christian God, whom she had worshipped with so much fervour in her parish in the Northamptonshire countryside, and who was once the source of her greatest happiness, ceased, also in a moment, to have any meaning. Panic. "She was terrified over an area larger than usual; the universe, never comprehensible to her intellect, offered no repose to her soul."

For Mrs. Moore there is no re-establishment from what befell her on the Marabar. Soon afterwards she leaves India. By her own estimate her passage to that land has been a failure. As she crosses the country by train to go aboard at Bombay she thinks "I have not seen the right places." The voice of the Marabar Caves was not the voice of India, only one of the voices; but it had prevented her hearing the others. The voice of Asirgarh, for instance, a fortress among wooded hills passed at sunset. She at once forgets Asirgarh; but ten minutes later Asirgarh reappears—the train has made a semicircle. "What could she connect it with, except its own name? Nothing; she knew no one who lived there. But it had looked at her twice and seemed to say: 'I do not vanish.' " On the passage home, she dies, and her body is committed to the Indian Ocean. She will never hear the voice of Asirgarh again; but Asirgarh will hear hers.

The goblins are powerful in this novel, but before the dark second part ends Forster begins to put them to rout. It is true that Mrs. Moore could not cope with what the caves had spoken to her. But, like Mrs. Wilcox, she is a redemptive character; unable to save herself, she did miraculous things for others. She did them by being the sort of person she was. She continued to do them after her ordeal at the Marabar. Whenever Adela Quested is in her company, and only then, Adela is relieved of the echo, and becomes not her usual self, but at times a better self than she has ever been. The mention of Mrs. Moore's name at the trial clears the confusion from Adela's brain, and in this way Aziz is saved. A little later the mention of her name to Aziz persuades him to be generous with Adela and give over an action for damages. And the beneficent influence of Mrs. Moore flowing out of the secret understanding of the heart will swell throughout the third part until it becomes next to the main determinant in the final scenes of the novel.

Even in the second part, the dark part of the novel, the goblins encounter another powerful enemy in the

Brahman Godbole. He is asked by Fielding for his opinion of what occurred in the cave. The breadth of his conception brings a quietude that reassures the reader if it leaves Fielding exasperated. What happened, says Godbole, was an evil thing. But the precise nature of the evil is not of any real account: nothing is to be achieved through the law courts, by ascertaining whether Aziz attacked Adela Quested, or whether someone else, the guide or a wandering Pathan, attacked her, or whether she was attacked by her own poisoned imagination. What concerns Godbole is why she was attacked. Evil had the power to attack her because of the shortcomings of the universe, because, to take an example of the shortcomings—this is my example, not Godbole's—of the warped society in which Adela and Aziz are living. Perhaps if the cave had been in Wiltshire or in Greece, Aziz and Adela might have left it unscathed. "When evil occurs," says Godbole, "it expresses the whole of the universe." But if all have a responsibility for letting the goblins loose, the power of the goblins is no proper reason for despair. Evil is not unrelated to good: it is the absence of good, and thus has a subtle unbreakable bond with the good. The presence of evil does not imply that good has been vanquished, only that it has receded. Godbole is also concerned with what should be done; not at the trial of Aziz, which, like Mrs. Moore, he will not take seriously, but in the effort to make good return. It is right, Godbole thinks, indeed it is imperative, that we continue our plea to God that He "come," that good may return and evil recede before it. Even so intimate a friend of the author as Lowes Dickinson was impatient to know what did occur in the cave; Forster never

offers even a hint, and we must thus conclude that like
Godbole and Mrs. Moore he is concerned, and wants
us to be concerned, not with what happened, but only
with why it happened and with what could and should
be done to assure and speed the recession of evil and
the return of good.

The third part of the novel is Godbole's until it becomes also Mrs. Moore's. Godbole leads the mysterious
ceremony of Hindu worship with which this last part
opens. The temple where he dances and prays, smears
his forehead with butter and tries to swallow the butter
as it trickles down his face and the faces of his friends,
is not in Chandrapore; it lies outside the strains of
British India, in a small native state a few miles only
from the fortress of Asirgarh. If the ceremony violates
all Western feelings about proportion and religious
decorum, we are brought to understand that the viola-
tion of proportion and religious decorum is the very
circumstance that enables the ceremony to intensify
the spiritual being of the worshippers. Godbole achieves
union with the divine, he propels Mrs. Moore and the
wasp into this union, he routs the goblins, because in
his worship he makes no fixed exclusions, he does not
exclude humour, he does not exclude ugliness. Everything but evil becomes the ally of good. So powerful is
the effect of this worship that even the non-Hindus in
the native state find their spiritual being intensified.

The next scene is theirs. Aziz takes Ralph Moore on
the water to witness the last stage in the Hindu ceremony. Fielding and Stella Moore, his wife, are in another boat. The four non-Hindus are intent on the ceremony unrolling by the shore. A raft is launched bearing
a clay god, who is to melt in the water. Suddenly the

two boats are very close to the raft and to each other. From the Hindus lining the shore comes a howl, whether of wrath or of joy no one else can tell, but it is reassuring that Godbole is there. Stella leans first towards her husband, then with an instinctive recognition of affinity that is among the most delicate and moving touches in the novel, she leans towards Aziz. The strange and unexpected gesture leads the two boats to overturn in the shallow water, after colliding with the raft. The god and his earthen retinue are involved in the confusion and the clay melts into mud. Meanwhile with a volume and complexity that reminds one of Forster's description of the close of the Fifth Symphony, guns roar, elephants trumpet, and like a mallet beating on a dome comes one crack of thunder loud enough to drown all else. A part of the god's retinue, now turned to mud, is swept back to shore and Godbole happily smears it on his forehead. The goblins are routed. All are one. The spirit of the ceremony with which this third part began reappears, to affect all the personages. Even a letter from Adela Quested, and another from Ronnie Heaslop, which had confirmed Aziz in his suspicions, float in the water with the sacred clay. The passage to India is over, and it has not been a failure. One of the voices of India that Mrs. Moore had not heard has spoken with trenchant power, and strangely her own voice has spoken in unison with it.

But no, the passage is not quite over. In Helen Schlegel's elucidation of the Fifth Symphony it was said that the goblins were still there. "They could return. He had said so bravely, and that is why one can trust Beethoven when he says other things." Forster too will say bravely that the goblins could return. The last ride together of the two friends Aziz and Fielding is a proof of the force and the fineness of the revived friendship; but it also shows how precarious their personal understanding was, how impotent they were to maintain it equably, how dependent it was on aid drawn from above themselves, from the Brahman Godbole, from Mrs. Moore.

Three big blocks of sound—that was Forster's account of rhythm in the Fifth Symphony. Three big blocks of sound—that is what *A Passage to India* consists of. A first block in which evil creeps about weakly, and the secret understanding of the heart is easily dominant. A second block, very long, and very dark, in which evil streams forth from the caves and lays waste almost everything about, but yet meets an opposition, indecisive in some ways, but unyielding, in the contemplative insight of Professor Godbole, and the intuitive fidelity of Mrs. Moore. A third block in which evil is forced to recede, summarily, and spectacularly, not by the secret understanding of the heart, but by the strength on which the secret understanding of the heart depends, contemplative insight, intuitive fidelity. Then the final reminder, that good has merely obliged evil to recede as good receded before evil a little before.

Reduced to the barest terms, the structure of *A Passage to India* has the "rhythmic rise-fall-rise" that Forster found in what has been for him, early and late, the greatest of novels, *War and Peace*.

IV

It is time, and perhaps rather more than time, to ask how the varied kinds of repetition with variation that

abound in *A Passage to India* aid that book in producing
its effect. A question that is difficult, perhaps impossible,
but it must be asked. It is so difficult because the effect
of *A Passage to India* is not a simple one, as the effect
of *The Old Wives' Tale* or *Vanity Fair* is simple. Forster's
imaginative sympathies have outrun his intellectual
commitments, and when this happens to a novelist the
result is either a confusion or a fine complexity. Forster's
intellectual commitments are clearly set out in his
pamphlet *What I Believe*. "My law givers are Erasmus
and Montaigne, not Moses and St. Paul." And again:
"Tolerance, good temper and sympathy—they are what
matter really." The person in *A Passage to India* who
has the best combination of tolerance, good temper, and
sympathy, who would be most likely to take Erasmus
and Montaigne as law givers, is Cyril Fielding. But *A
Passage to India* is not conceived according to Fielding's
liberal, sceptical, humanist values. It is conceived according to values much better apprehended by Mrs.
Moore, who is irritable, of uncertain sympathies, in her
time of crisis acridly intolerant, and who quotes only
one author—St. Paul. It should not be too much of a
disturbance in interpreting a novel to find the artist's
imaginative sympathies outrunning his intellectual commitments— even so temperate an artist as Turgenev had
it happen to him in rendering Bazarov in *Fathers and
Sons.*

The main effect in *A Passage to India* is, I believe, of
order in the universe, but order that can be merely
glimpsed, never seized for sure. In the poem from
which the title comes, Whitman ends by bidding us

steer for the deep waters only,
Reckless O soul, exploring, I with thee, and thou with me,

For we are bound where mariner has not yet dared to go,
And we will risk the ship, ourselves and all.

O my brave soul!
O farther farther sail!
O daring joy, but safe! are they not all the seas of God?
O farther, farther, farther sail.

It is because they are exploring in the seas of God that
Mrs. Moore is not deluded in respecting the admonition
of Asirgarh "I do not vanish"; that Godbole is not deluded when among the circling images he is led to
propel Mrs. Moore and the wasp towards the divine.
They move in mystery, but the mystery is not a muddle.
It is an order.

To express what is both an order and a mystery
rhythmic processes, repetitions with intricate variations,
are the most appropriate of idioms. Repetition is the
strongest assurance an author can give of order; the
extraordinary complexity of the variations is the reminder that the order is so involute that it must remain
a mystery. *A Passage to India* is a prophetic novel, a
singing in the halls of fiction: the infinite resourcefulness
of Forster has given it a rhythmic form that enables us
to respond to it as prophecy and song; to pass beyond
character, story, and setting, and attend, delightedly,
to the grouping and ungrouping of ideas and emotions;
to feel that numinous element so constantly present in
the experience of the great man whom in these discourses I have wished to honour.

INDEX

A la recherche du temps perdu, 35–41, 43–46
Ambassadors, The, 24–27
Aspects of the Novel, 3, 7, 25, 35, 41, 43–46, 57–58, 63–64, 84–85

Balzac, Honoré de, 20–23, 92
Bardèche, Maurice, 10
Beach, Joseph Warren, 15
Beauchamp's Career, 41
Bennett, Arnold, 16–18, 114
Bergson, Henri, 10
Blackstone, Bernard, 65, 69
Bridge of San Luis Rey, The, 42–43
Brontë, Emily, 6, 57
Brontë, Patrick, 6
Brothers Karamazov, The, 58
Butler, Samuel, 33, 86

Cakes and Ale, 4–5
Carlyle, Thomas, 56
Cather, Willa, 35, 71–78, 85
Compton-Burnett, Ivy, 22
Conrad, Joseph, 27
Craft of Fiction, The, 3, 24

Dandieu, Arnaud, 41
Death Comes for the Archbishop, 71
Death in Venice, 70
Dickens, Charles, 48
Dickinson, G. Lowes, 110
Dostoevski, F. M., 58

Eliot, George, 9–11, 86
En route, 3
Esther Waters, 11–13, 89, 92

Fathers and Sons, 114
Flaubert, Gustave, 33–34

Forster, Edward Morgan, 3, 7, 25, 35, 41, 43–55, 57–58, 63, 84–85, 86, 89–115

Grave, The, 76
Great Expectations, 48

Hardy, Thomas, 13–16
Hero of Our Times, A, 86
Howards End, 46–55, 92–93, 105, 108
Huxley, Aldous, 8–9, 13, 45
Huysmans, Joris Karl, 3

James, Henry, 4, 24–27, 34
Joyce, James, 7

Lathrop, H. B., 18
Lear of the Steppes, A, 23–24, 92
Legouis, Emile, 6
Lermontov, M. Y., 86
Longest Journey, The, 46, 53–54, 56, 70
Longfellow, Henry Wadsworth, 76
Lubbock, Percy, 3, 24

Madame Bovary, 33, 34
Magic Mountain, The, 70
Mann, Thomas, 4, 70–71
Marquand, J. P., 33
Maugham, W. Somerset, 4–5
Melville, Herman, 52
Meredith, George, 41
Middlemarch, 9–11, 86
Moby Dick, 52
Moore, George, 11–13, 89, 92
Muir, Edwin, 35

Newcomes, The, 19

Old Wives' Tale, The, 16–18, 114
Oliphant, Mrs. M. L. W., 28–29

Passage to India, A, 63–64, 86, 89–115
Paul, Elliot, 7
Père Goriot, Le, 20–23, 92
Point Counter Point, 8–9, 13, 45
Porterfield, Alexander, 71–72
Portrait of a Lady, 34
Professor's House, The, 35, 71–78, 85
Proust, Marcel, 35–41, 43–46, 51–55

Room with a View, A, 46, 53–54
Ruskin, John, 55

Scott, Sir Walter, 10
Sesame and Lilies, 55
Sterne, Laurence, 6
Stoll, Elmer Edgar, 10
Summing Up, The, 5

Thackeray, W. M., 18–20, 34, 114
Tolstoy, Leo, 56, 78–85
To the Lighthouse, 64–70, 85
Tristram Shandy, 6
Trollope, Anthony, 55–56
Turgenev, I. S., 23–24, 92, 114
Two Worlds and Their Ways, 22

Ulysses, 7–8

Vanity Fair, 18–20, 114
Vigneron, Robert, 35
Virginians, The, 34

Wagner, Richard, 28, 56
War and Peace, 56, 64, 78–85
Way of All Flesh, The, 33, 86
Well-Beloved, The, 13–16
What I Believe, 114
Wilder, Thornton, 42–43
Woolf, Virginia, 33, 64–70, 85
Wuthering Heights, 6, 57

Zola, Emile, 3, 28